Better Homes and Gardens®

# ENERGY-SAVING PROJECTS
## YOU CAN BUILD

W9-CPG-173

**BETTER HOMES AND GARDENS® BOOKS**

Editor in Chief: James A. Autry
Editorial Director: Neil Kuehnl
Executive Art Director: William J. Yates

Editor: Gerald M. Knox
Art Director: Ernest Shelton
Associate Art Director: Randall Yontz
Copy and Production Editors: David Kirchner,
Lamont Olson, David A. Walsh
Senior Graphic Designer: Harijs Priekulis
Graphic Designers: Faith Berven,
Sheryl Veenschoten, Richard Lewis,
Neoma Alt West, Linda Ford, Thomas Wegner

Building and Remodeling Editor: Noel Seney
Building Books Editor: Larry Clayton

*Energy-Saving Projects You Can Build*
Editors: Noel Seney, Larry Clayton
Copy and Production Editor: David A. Walsh
Graphic Designers: Randall Yontz, Doris Meacham
Contributing Writers: Victor D. Chase, John Sculley
Project Designs: David Ashe, William C. Schuster,
Steven Mead, and Lynch, Payne, Champion, Bernabe, A.I.A.
Exploded Drawings: William C. Schuster
Illustrations: Hellman Design Associates,
Graphic Center

# CONTENTS

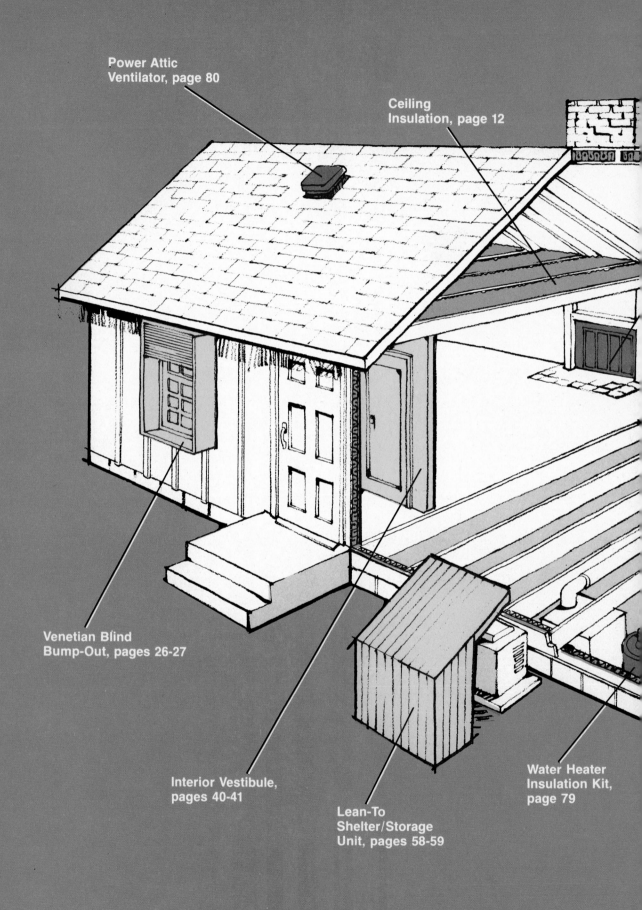

Power Attic
Ventilator, page 80

Ceiling
Insulation, page 12

Venetian Blind
Bump-Out, pages 26-27

Interior Vestibule,
pages 40-41

Lean-To
Shelter/Storage
Unit, pages 58-59

Water Heater
Insulation Kit,
page 79

Glass Fireplace
Doors, page 77

Attic
Insulation, page 12

No Frills
Skylight Cover,
page 75

Insulating Shutters,
pages 40-41

Awning-Type
Sunshade, page 29

Insulating
Above-Grade
Walls, page 18

# HOW TO GET STARTED

Saving energy, as with most things around your home, is a matter of understanding the problem and your own situation, and of coming up with a plan of action. This book will help you do just that by giving you the know-how to get going.

Visualize your home the way we've sketched this one. At first, it may seem a bit overwhelming; however, if you look at the things you need to do as individual projects, you'll find the task much easier.

The energy-saving ideas shown here all follow the four sections of this book:
● Energy-Saving Basics (shown in orange): These are all the primary ingredients of an energy-efficient house. Look to these areas first because they offer the most fuel-saving potential.
● Projects You Can Build (shown in yellow): These are big and little problem solvers that help eliminate wasted energy both winter and summer.
● Energy-Saving Products For You (shown in red): These are all worthwhile investments that help save money without sacrificing comfort.
● Your Heating and Cooling Equipment: This section looks at your equipment and tells how to keep it in tip-top shape.

# GETTING
# STARTED
# (CONTINUED)

**Energy-Saving Basics:** Get your teeth into this section of the book first. It gives the information you need to help establish how much insulation you have in your house, for instance, and how much you should have. Then you'll learn how to install insulation yourself in the areas where it will do the most good. You'll also learn what insulating jobs you shouldn't tackle yourself.

Knowing what you can do easily, such as applying caulking compounds and weather stripping to add to your comfort, you can set up a plan to work on your own insulating program from the top of your house to the bottom.

Projects in this section that plug up energy leaks offer the biggest money-saving potential for most families. If your house is more than 15 or 20 years old, you'll find the payoff is relatively high for the dollars and the effort you'll be investing. Even if your house is newer than that, you can use the information in this section to check the adequacy of its insulation. Then you'll be ready to "fine tune" your home with the ideas and projects in the sections that follow.

**Projects You Can Build:** This section contains a wide assortment of projects that were all especially designed to help you solve particular energy problems at your house. There are solutions for both winter and summer. You'll find ways to block out the hot summer sun, as well as ways to keep the blustery winter winds away from your door.

For all the projects, there are exploded-view drawings of how the projects go together, step-by-step instructions, and illustrations that will help you decide what your projects will look like. Of course, you'll need to adapt the projects you select to fit your house. Feel free to change the sizes for your own situation, change the materials to blend with others you already have, and embellish the projects or strip them down.

As you pick and choose those projects that will do the best energy-saving job for you, be sure you consider the extras they offer. Some also add outdoor living opportunities; some bring extra privacy; others add storage; and many enhance the exterior appearance of your house.

**Energy-Saving Products for You:** The marketplace today offers a wide range of energy-saving products, and many of them are quite worthwhile. We've selected a group that comprises the better products to help you reduce fuel bills.

This section also will help you decide which products will do more for your family and how to shop to get the features you want. Also, you'll get a good insight into what's involved in the installation of each product. However, for all of the products discussed, you can expect more-detailed installation instructions from the manufacturer. These procedures vary from one brand to another, so be sure to review the steps required before you buy a specific product.

As with all the other ideas in this book, use common sense in the selection of the products we describe. First, you'll want to balance the savings you might expect against the investment involved. Then, add the comfort and convenience that many of the products offer. And, of course, when that balance is on the plus side for you, the sooner you get going, the better.

**Heating and Cooling Equipment:** With the information included in this section, you'll understand how all of your heating and cooling equipment works. Detailed drawings show what's inside various types of furnaces, air conditioners, and heat pumps. Plus, we've included all the things you can do to maintain your system properly—even little adjustments can often make a big difference.

This section also helps you understand how the proper humidity level means more comfort, winter or summer. In winter, for instance, adding moisture to the air in your house often can make you feel comfortable at a lower temperature than is possible with air that is too dry.

Also, you'll find information to help you with the care and management of your thermostat. You'll be able to understand how it functions so you can keep it set at the point that works best for your own situation. Plus, there are complete details on cleaning various types—you'll see how to take yours apart, put it in tip-top shape, and reassemble for optimum performance.

# ENERGY-SAVING BASICS

Eliminate your worst energy-wasters first, and your payoff will be the greatest—in both money and energy saved. Then eliminate your house's minor energy ills on a case-by-case basis to make it truly energy efficient.

## INSULATION ABCs

Adequate insulation is the foremost step in conserving energy. And the subject is not as bewildering as it may seem. When you start shopping, you'll find four basic types of insulation products, which are shown in the chart.

**Batts and Blankets (A):** These are made of flexible material such as fiber glass. They come in standard widths to fit between studs and joists, and are the easiest of the basic types of insulation to use where you have access to these structural members. Batts are 48 inches long.

Blankets come in longer rolls and can be purchased with an attached vapor barrier that prevents moisture damage. The vapor barrier has flanges for stapling to the structure, also.

**Loose Fill (B):** This category consists of several types of mineral fibers (glass wool, slag wool, and rock wool) and cellulose, which is composed of recycled newspapers or wood chips.

These insulations can be poured into accessible spaces or blown into inaccessible spaces, such as under floors, or behind walls. Loose fill insulation does have limitations, however. Also, it may not be very effective if blown into walls where there are obstructions or where some insulation already exists.

Mineral fiber insulation is not a fire hazard; however, cellulose insulation has had problems with flammability. It can be chemically treated to retard flammability, but this treatment is not always foolproof.

If you use cellulose, you should look at the label on the bag (or, if the insulation work is done by a contractor, ask him about the insulation he will be blowing into your home) to check its flammability rating. Look for an Underwriters Laboratories (UL) classification label. Such a label doesn't mean that UL approves the insulation, only that it has tested it.

On this label will be a rating between 0 and 100—the lower the number the more fire resistant the material. Once you have the number, ask your local building officials whether the number on the bag is in keeping with the requirements of your local building code. Recent federal legislation requires a rating of 0 to 25 for cellulose insulation.

**Foam Insulation (C):** There are two types in this category: polyurethane and ureaformaldehyde. These materials solidify after being pumped into place. Polyurethane has a high R-value; however, it expands after being injected, and the results could be disastrous if that happens inside your walls. Ureaformaldehyde, on the other hand, is injected at its full size and can be shot into existing closed walls. While it cures it gives off a harmful odor that must be properly vented. Also, holes through which it is injected must be left open for a required period of time to allow for proper curing.

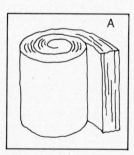 A
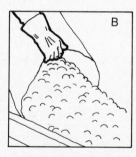 B
 C
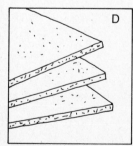 D

| R-Values per Inch of Thickness | | | |
|---|---|---|---|
| Fiberglass R-3.1 | Mineral Fibers R-3.1 | Polyurethane R-6.2 | Urethane R-6 |
| | Cellulose R-3.7 | Ureaformaldehyde R-4.5 | Polystyrene R-5 |
| | | | Polyisocyanurate R-8 |

There are indications that this material might shrink after installation. This could reduce its effectiveness. Also, its injection into walls is a process that requires considerable skill, so make sure the contractor you hire knows what he is doing.

**Rigid Insulation (D):** There are three forms in this group; Urethane, polystyrene, and polyisocyanurate. They are all widely used in new construction and are most commonly used to insulate the inside of basement walls. And, if you're planning to re-side your house, you can use this type of insulation under the new siding.

Urethane and polystyrene give off toxic fumes when burning and most codes, as well as common sense, dictate that they must not be left exposed to a home's living spaces. When used on the inside of basement walls, for example, they should be covered with gypsum board at least ½-inch thick.

Polyisocyanurate, however, has been approved for exposed internal use and does not need to be covered with gypsum board. With the exception of the gypsum board covering, all three are installed the same way.

## R-Value = Effectiveness

The standard measure of the effectiveness of any insulation is its resistance to heat flow, called "R-value." The higher the R-value, the better an insulator the material is. The chart of the various types of insulating materials shown at left gives the R-value for each type per inch of thickness.

However, not all materials come in one-inch increments; for example, fiber-glass blankets usually are made in 1-, 3½-, and 6-inch thicknesses.

Comparing R-values will help you choose between products—and in talking to contractors.

## How much is enough?

This is a complex question with a precise answer that depends on where you live, on the heating and cooling equipment you have, and on the cost of fuel and electricity in your city. The map below is a general guideline and will help you in your preliminary planning.

Find your location and note the zone. Typical R-value requirements for each zone are shown below the map. The three numbers in the ratings indicate the insulation ratings you should have for your ceiling, your floor, and your outside walls. If you live in zone five, for instance, you should strive for R-33 in ceilings, R-19 in floors, and R-22 in walls.

Nearly all public utility companies can give you a more precise recommendation for your location. These recommendations take local heating and cooling rates into consideration as well as unusual climate conditions.

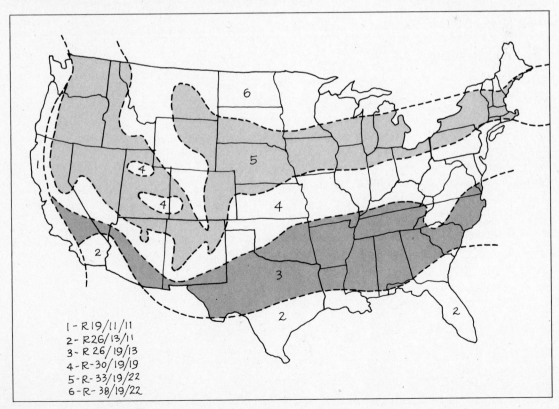

1 - R19/11/11
2 - R26/13/11
3 - R26/19/13
4 - R-30/19/19
5 - R-33/19/22
6 - R-38/19/22

# VENTILATION AND VAPOR

The benefits of adding insulation are well known and understood by most homeowners. Less well known—but equally important to maintaining a sound, energy-conserving home—is the need for proper control of moisture with vapor barriers and ventilation.

Uncontrolled vapor can seriously reduce the effectiveness of most kinds of insulation. Vapor also can harm the structural parts of a house. And, the more insulation that one adds to a house, the greater a problem uncontrolled vapor can be. It is, therefore, essential that insulation be installed properly and that other steps be taken to control any moisture problems.

Here's how moisture gets to be a problem: Water, in the form of vapor, normally passes through both the walls and ceilings of

your home as the structure "breathes." In the wintertime, the air within the walls is much colder than the air inside the house. Since cold air can't hold as much moisture as warm air, the vapor condenses to water as it is deposited on—and freezes to—the insulation and wood structural members in a wall. In the attic, ice often forms on the underside of the roof and the supporting rafters. Then, when the weather warms up, this ice melts. The result can be water damage. Even a single wetting of most insulations will seriously decrease their effectiveness. Structural members may rot over a period of time when wetness occurs.

## Installing a Vapor Barrier

Step one in controlling moisture is putting in a vapor barrier. Such a barrier is basically non-porous and resists the passage of vapor. You can buy fiber-glass batts and

blankets with a vapor barrier of heavy kraft paper attached to them. This paper has flanges on it so that it can be stapled to the joists of studs, holding both it and the insulation in place.

Some fiber-glass insulation comes with a foil backing. This is a vapor barrier and has the advantage of reflecting heat.

If you install loose fill insulation, use a thin sheet of plastic film (polyethylene) as a vapor barrier. Polyethylene film also can be used in conjunction with batts and blankets that do not come with barriers. Rigid plastic foam board insulations act as their own vapor barriers.

The most important thing to remember about vapor barriers is that they must always be applied facing the inside of the house (the warm side in winter). In other words, if you are pouring loose fill insulation on the attic floor, the vapor barrier must be laid before the insulation is poured. With products that have a built-in bar-

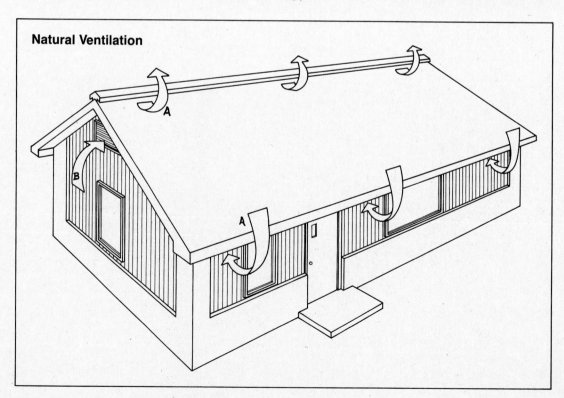

**Natural Ventilation**

rier, that side must go face down, against the top of the ceiling.

Should there already be some insulation in place, don't lay insulation with a vapor barrier on top of it. You can trap moisture in the insulation between the ceiling and the vapor barrier. Move aside the old insulation, and put down the new with the vapor barrier, then add the old on top of the new. Or, if the old insulation has a vapor barrier, add new insulation without a vapor barrier.

## Ventilating Attic Spaces

Good attic ventilation is essential for two reasons. First, it helps reduce moisture buildup in winter. Second, it helps remove hot air in the summer—which helps reduce the air conditioning load. Without attic ventilation, there is always some chance of moisture condensation in the winter, even with a good vapor barrier and insulation. A flow of cold out-side air will prevent this. In the summer, unvented attics will tend to heat up from the sun's beating on the roof. The result is that air conditioning equipment has to work harder and use more energy. There are two answers: natural and forced ventilation.

## Natural Ventilation

This method depends on the tendency of hot air to rise and move fresh air through the attic. The best natural ventilation can be provided by openings at the ridge of the roof and the eaves of your house (A). The arrows show how air will flow in the eaves and out the top, very naturally. Or, openings in the gabled ends of the attic can provide an outlet for the air coming in from the eaves. Less effective, but better than no venting at all, are louvered openings in both gable ends (B). Breezes change the air inside the attic by blowing in one opening and out the other.

## Forced Ventilation

A better way to provide good ventilation is to use a power unit. This is a ventilator with an electric motor and fan that can be mounted on the roof near the ridge (C) or that can be installed in an opening in the gable end of the attic (D). These are especially effective for summer use to prevent heat buildup. These fans can be thermostatically controlled so they operate automatically.

Both types need inlets, of course. Eave vents (E) are best for the roof-mounted type, although openings in the gable ends are often satisfactory. For fans installed in a gable, you can provide a louvered opening (F) in the opposite end for the intake.

Power ventilation can be especially valuable to help boost the natural convection flow of air in homes with large roof areas (where gable end vents are more than 50 feet apart, for example, and there is no ridge vent).

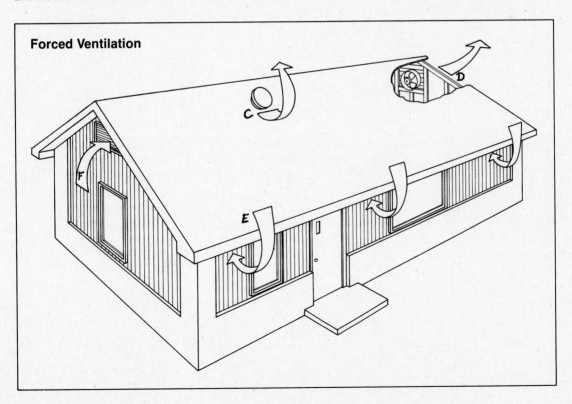

Forced Ventilation

# INSULATING CEILINGS AND ATTICS

The attic space in your house is an excellent place to begin your energy-saving program. First, the attic is usually very easily accessible. Second, insulating this area makes good economic sense. You'll block the heat from rising out of the living space below in the wintertime. In summer, the insulation will help reduce the air conditioning load. If your attic is an unfinished one, you can add insulation by placing it directly on top of the ceiling. Be sure to take a wide board or piece of plywood to walk and work on. The board should be long enough to stretch across several joists so that your weight is spread evenly. Never step or brace yourself on the ceiling itself; you might go through it.

Where the attic is unfinished, but has a floor, you can lift the flooring, insert the insulation, then replace the flooring. Or you might call in a professional insulator who will lift a few boards between each joist and blow loose-fill insulation into the cavities.

If you are considering finishing the attic into an extra bedroom, there is no real problem. Just insulate the walls of the attic with blanket insulation.

The first step is to take a look in your attic to see how much, if any, insulation is there. While you're up there, see whether a vapor barrier is in place, and check the amount of ventilation you have. Then determine how much insulation you should have, and select the type of insulation you want to use (see pages 8 and 9). It is an excellent idea to check with your supplier of building materials before making any firm decisions. You may find certain kinds of insulation, such as fiber-glass blankets, in short supply. He also can help determine how much material you will need to buy to achieve the thickness you have decided is necessary to properly insulate your attic.

Because insulation can irritate skin, eyes, and lungs, you'll need some protective equipment, too. When working with fiber-glass in-

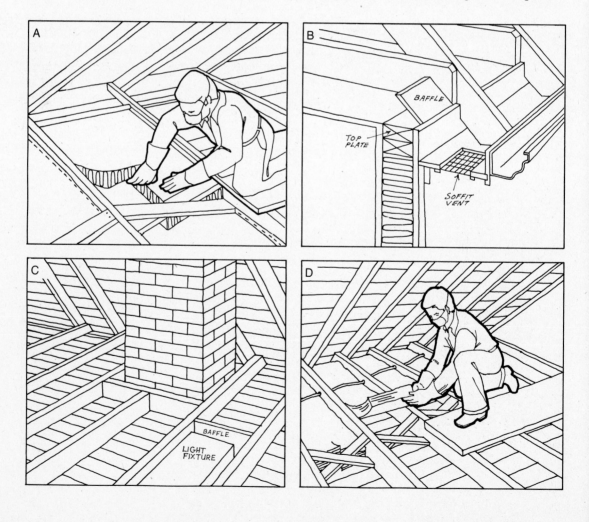

sulation you should wear gloves and long sleeves. A dust mask and goggles also are good items to have whenever you work with insulation.

## Adding Ceiling Insulation

If you choose to insulate the ceiling with loose-fill insulation (or if you choose batt or blanket insulation without a vapor barrier), the first step you need to take is to put a vapor barrier in place. Use polyethylene film and staple it every few inches for a tight seal. Be sure that you overlap or tape the seams between sheets to prevent any vapor leaks. If you choose a blanket-type product with a barrier, just fit it (vapor barrier side down) between the joists (A).

If you're going to use loose-fill insulation, attach a baffle between all the joists to keep the insulation from drifting onto and blocking the soffit vents (B). Also, nail baffles around all light fixtures that protrude through the ceiling (C). For batts or blankets, just cut them three inches short of the fixtures. If you want to insulate over the fixture, plan a framework to provide a 24-inch clearance above the fixture.

Now continue either pouring or laying the insulation. If you use blankets, pass them under wiring wherever possible (D). Also, cut the pieces a little long and place the ends tightly against the top plate. When using loose-fill, make sure all gaps between joists are filled by smoothing the insulation with a board (E).

## Insulating Attic Walls

If you intend to finish off the attic, plan the insulation this way. Start by nailing collar beams to the rafters at the planned ceiling height (F). Use insulating blankets that have a vapor barrier to make the installation easier for you. Cut blankets to length for placing between the rafters and the collar beams, and staple through the flanges (G). Then tape the joints between the blankets (H) to prevent vapor from passing through. Insulate the end walls—just staple blankets to the studs.

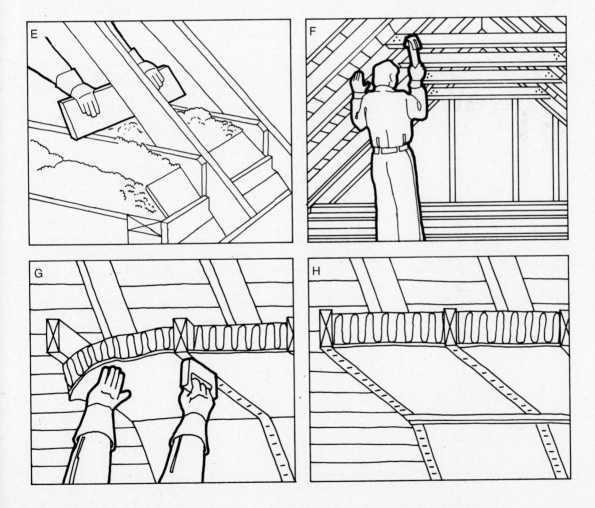

# INSULATING BASEMENT WALLS

The colder your climate and the more your basement walls extend above the frost line, the wiser it is for you to insulate basement walls. And, this project has a built-in bonus—only a little more effort is needed for a finished wall surface. So, you can upgrade the basement to living or play space in the bargain.

## Getting Ready

The first thing in preparing for a basement insulation job is to make sure the walls of your basement are dry. If water seeps in, it can render the insulation useless. So you must stop any leaks first.

While you're in the planning stage, don't forget about electrical outlets. Run outlets to wherever you'll want them. Make sure you extend them far enough out from the existing wall so they'll match the plane of the new wall. Then, when you are installing the insulation, try to pack a piece of blanket behind the wiring outlets and pipes (A).

## Installing Blankets

If you choose to use blankets to insulate your basement, it is necessary to put up some sort of frame to which the insulation and drywall or paneling can be attached. There are two ways to go. One is to put furring strips in place (B). You can use masonry nails, or you can opt for the somewhat easier route of using a construction adhesive made just for this.

The thickness of the insulation you'll be using will determine the size of the furring strips you need. For one-inch-thick blankets (R-7) with an attached vapor barrier, use 2x2 furring strips. For 3½-inch blankets (R-11) with a vapor barrier, attach 2x4s. In either case, put the flanges of the vapor barrier over the furring strips and staple them securely in place.

You also can use blanket insulation without a vapor barrier. This can be friction-fit between the fur-

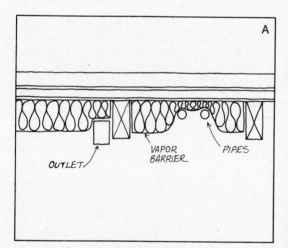

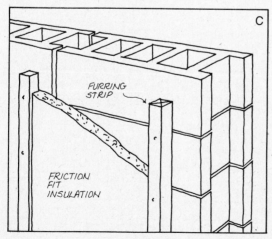

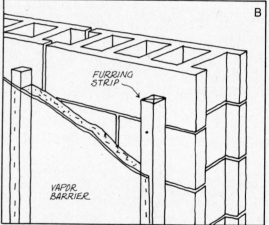

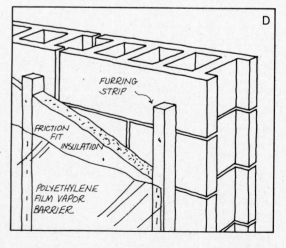

ring strips (C). Then you should install a polyethylene film vapor barrier over it (D).

The other way to go about preparing for blanket insulation is to build a full frame with horizontal top and bottom plates and vertical studs (E). The insulation goes between the studs just as with the furring strips.

An important note on spacing: Whether you are using furring strips, or a full frame, plan the vertical members with either 16- or 24-inch center-to-center spacing because the blankets come in sizes to fit between these standard widths.

After the insulation is in place, you can finish off the basement by attaching drywall or paneling to the furring strips or studs.

## Installing Rigid Foam Panels

Lightweight foam panels provide another way to go. They offer greater R-values per inch. Polystyrene and polyurethane types must be covered with gypsum drywall at least ½ inch thick. Polyisocyanurate panels don't require covering, but you may want to apply it for appearance.

The only framework you need is horizontal wood nailing strips along the top and bottom of the masonry wall (F). Make these nailers two inches wide and the thickness of the panels. For most basements, 1x2-inch nailers with ¾-inch insulation board will suffice. However, if your region is especially cold, or if you have a

walk-out basement, opt for 1-inch-thick insulation. Rip 2x4s to get nailers the right thickness.

Now that you're ready to put up the panels, work with one at a time. To fit around surface projections and openings, score the material with a utility knife, then snap the panel. Apply ribbons of mastic and simply press the board into place (G). Place the boards horizontally or vertically.

Then apply the gypsum drywall in much the same way, cutting and fitting as you go. Nail the drywall top and bottom, finish the joints and add moldings (H). Add texture to the surface if you like, and paint. Or, install pre-finished paneling over the drywall. You can nail it or use adhesive with equally good results.

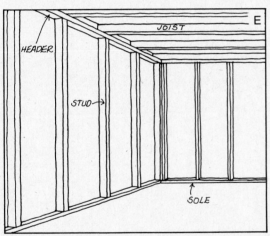

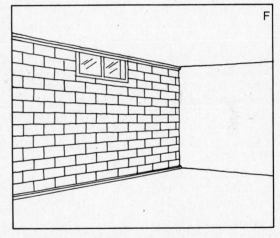

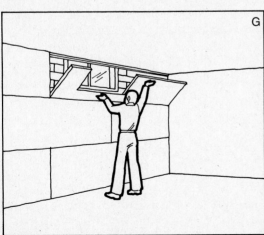

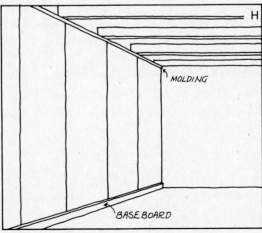

# INSULATING FLOORS AND FOUNDATIONS

It is not uncommon to overlook crawl spaces, floors, and foundations when it comes to planning an insulation program. These are parts of your house that you rarely look at; however, don't underestimate the importance of insulating these areas because the investment can save you money.

The right way to do it depends on the construction of your home. If you have a heated crawl space, plan to insulate the inside of the foundation walls of the crawl space. There are a few exceptions to this rule, however. In areas of extreme cold, such as Minnesota and Alaska, this insulating method and the deep frost penetration can combine to cause foundation heaving. In such areas—and in houses with unheated crawl spaces—the floor over the crawl space should be insulated. If your program calls for insulating the walls of a heated crawl space, you should provide vent areas that you can open during the summer months.

If your house is built on a concrete slab, you should plan to insulate around the exterior perimeter of the foundation with a rigid foam insulation.

## Insulating a Heated Crawl Space

To insulate the walls of a crawl space, use flexible insulation with an attached vapor barrier. Remember, the vapor barrier goes toward the warm side in winter, meaning it should be installed so that it faces you and not the wall itself.

If the joists run at right angles to the foundation walls, begin by cutting and placing a piece of insulation on the sill plate and against the header (A). Now use strips of wood as nailers to secure the blankets to the sill plate so that the blankets fall against the foundation wall surface (B). You should cut the insulation long enough so that it will extend a minimum of two feet inward from the wall.

In situations where the joists run parallel to the wall it is not necessary to first cut short pieces to go against the header. Just tuck the blanket snugly against the header and floor, and attach (C). As you move along from blanket to blanket, make sure there are no spaces between them. If you do leave any cracks or openings, the effectiveness of the insulation will be reduced because the cold outside air will seep in.

Now it is time to spread a polyethylene film vapor barrier over the ground (D). This keeps the insulation from becoming wet and, therefore, less effective because of ground water or dampness. Be sure to put down the film only after you have nailed the blankets in place. If you put the film down first, you may tear holes in it as you work.

Lay the vapor barrier so that at least six inches of it rest against the foundation wall, up under the blankets. This will prevent moisture from creeping into the insulation at the point where the ground meets the wall. Also, place adjoining sheets of the plastic film so that one overlaps the next by six inches. Or, you can tape the edges of the sheets together very securely (E). Either way, you'll prevent leakage where the sheets come together.

Once the vapor barrier is in place, all you have to do is place 2x4s, rocks, bricks, or some heavy objects on the blankets to hold them in place against the foundation wall (F).

## Insulating A Floor

Almost any floor that is above an unheated space can be insulated rather easily with blanket insulation. The primary thing to remember here is that insulation you buy will have an attached vapor barrier, and the vapor barrier should be placed so that in wintertime it faces the warm area of your home. In this case it means the vapor barrier will face the underside of the floor—or away from you as you work.

The insulation can be held in place below the floor in a variety of ways. One way is to nail strips of wood across the joists (G). You can use laths, or rip narrow strips from scraps of wood you have on hand.

Another way to go is to staple chicken wire to joists (H). Apply a few feet of wire, and then slide the blankets in place above. Continue using this method until you have completed the installation.

Perhaps the simplest method is to support the insulation with friction-fit wires, forced up between the joists (I). Most insulation suppliers stock these wire supports, which are especially made for the job. You can just unroll the blankets, forcing the support wires in place where you need them as you go.

When you encounter pipes or other obstructions, measure to establish their location and mark that spot on the blanket. Next, cut a slot to the hole and remove just enough of the material to fit snugly against the obstruction (J). Then just slip the blanket in place around the pipe.

If you choose rigid-foam insulation, install it perpendicular to the joists (K). Apply mastic to the bottom surfaces of the joists and press planks or larger panels into place. As in the case of using this material on walls, you'll need to cover it with drywall. Nail the drywall to the floor joists above.

## Insulating a Concrete Slab

If your house is built on a slab, you may think cold floors are unavoidable and there's little you can do in the way of insulating the foundation. But it is possible to keep the cold from seeping in, although more work is involved in this situation than in houses with either basements or crawl spaces.

You can insulate the foundation around the slab by placing rigid foam insulating panels on the exterior of the foundation (L). Plan the depth of the insulation at least two feet, preferably to the frost line in your locality. You'll need to dig down to this point and brush off the foundation. Ask your insulation retailer for a special mastic (and read the label carefully) to stick the rigid board to the foundation. Place the insulation against the bottom of the siding and press in place. The final step is to replace the dirt you removed—it helps hold the insulation.

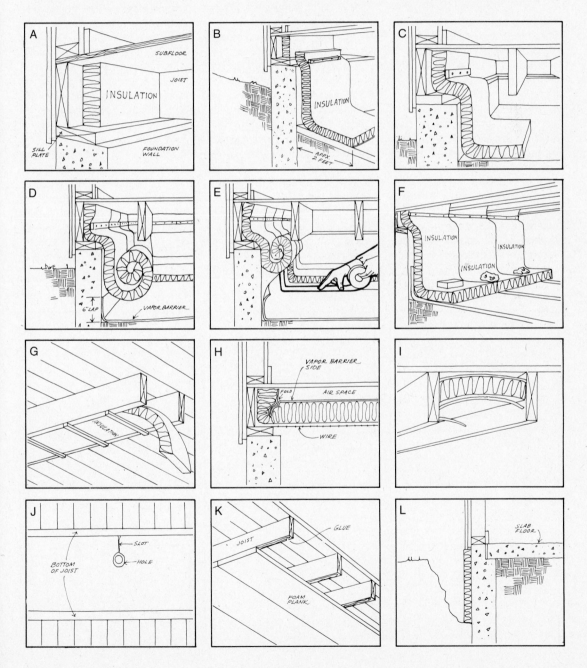

# INSULATING ABOVE-GRADE WALLS

When it comes to insulating the exterior walls of your home, there really isn't much a do-it-yourselfer can do unless you are planning extensive remodeling anyway. You may be able to peel off the inside or outside wall surface that will be replaced in the remodeling in order to get to the wall cavities. So although it's not impossible for an accomplished handyman to tackle above-grade walls, it's a job most homeowners should leave to the professional installers.

The problem is not all professionals use high-quality materials and the quality of their work varies. So, these pages will help you decide whether having the exterior walls insulated is the right move for you and will help give you a good foundation on which to select a professional insulation contractor should you decide to have insulation installed.

## How Much Insulation Do You Have?

The first question that must be answered when considering exterior wall insulation is how much, if any, you already have. This seemingly simple question is not always very easily answered. If your home is frame construction and was built from the latter part of the 1960s on, chances are your outside walls are reasonably well insulated.

Today it is the standard practice for builders to use 3½-inch blankets in the walls (A), which provide an R-11 insulation value. Before the late 1960s, in the days when energy was cheap and plentiful—and when edges were trimmed to cut building costs—insulation was one of the first things to go.

If your house was built during those earlier days, the exterior walls may have little or no insulation. If you have access to the plans of your house, take a look at them and they will tell you. Or, you may try to find the builder.

Another way to check is to look. If you have a basement that doesn't have a finished ceiling, shining a flashlight up into the exterior wall where a part of the cavity may be exposed can give you the answer. If not, try going up into the attic and looking down.

Sometimes, you can get a peek into the wall cavities by removing switch plates and outlet covers. Since this is such a simple job, it's worth a try, even though it is not always conclusive.

No openings? Then simply feel. It's best to do this during the wintertime when the temperature really drops outside. Feel the inside of one of your exterior walls. Then put your hand on an interior wall. If the exterior wall is considerably colder than the surface of

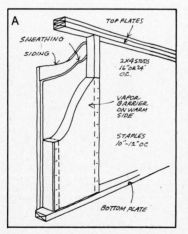

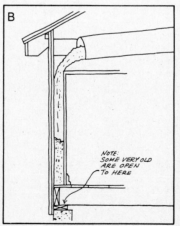

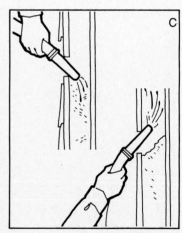

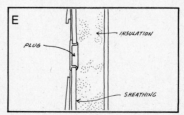

the inside wall, insulation probably is needed.

If none of these approaches answers the question, you'll have to cut a hole in the wall and look. It's fairly simple, but the repairing is tough enough to make a hole your last resort.

A cold wall not only robs heat from your home, but also makes you uncomfortable. When you sit near a cold wall, your body will radiate heat toward the cold surface. The result is that even though the air immediately around you is a comfortable temperature, you feel chilly. To compensate for that you turn up the thermostat, using more energy.

The point is, if the wall does feel cold, now is the time to take a serious look behind it to see what is there.

If, upon investigation, you find that there is *some* insulation in your exterior walls, you have a problem: It's very difficult to add insulation to partially insulated walls because the existing insu-

lation can block the new insulation from properly filling the cavity.

## Better Types Of Insulation

The more common methods of insulating existing, finished exterior walls are to have loose-fill insulation blown into the wall cavity (B), or ureaformaldehyde foam pumped into place (C). The foam, as it flows into the wall cavity where it solidifies, looks like shaving cream from an aerosol can.

## How They're Installed

Both types of insulation are installed through holes cut in either the exterior or interior of the walls (D). Usually, exterior installation is preferable since a hole has to be drilled to fill each of the spaces between the studs. If the drilling is done from the outside, once the holes are plugged (E) the shingles or siding can be replaced (F)

leaving little, if any, evidence of a repair.

Getting inside the wall if your house has brick veneer can be a little more difficult. Some brick walls have a removable facing board, making it easy to get to the framing. Where such a facing board is not available it may be less costly to drill holes on the inside of the wall. However, even with patching, these holes may be hard to disguise.

After drilling the holes, your contractor should check the cavities of the wall with a plumb bob to make sure there are no obstructions such as wires, fire stops, or pipes. These might block the flow of the insulation.

If you elect to have ureaformaldehyde foam pumped into your walls, be sure to discuss curing time with the contractor. This insulation gives off a noxious odor during the curing process, and proper venting is necessary. It's much better to be aware of the problem before he starts.

## Insulation contractor checklist

Here are seven points of discussion you'll want to keep in mind when you talk to a contractor about insulating any part of your house.
1. Track Record—You're generally better off to choose a company that is well known. Ask how long it has been in business, location of its building, and the like. The contractor also should offer a list of references and satisfied customers.
2. Consider R-value Only—Be sure that the contractor understands what R-value you have in mind. If he tends to cloud the issue with other benefits, be especially careful.
3. Product Liability Insurance and Workman's Compensation—The contractor should volunteer the fact that his firm is covered in both these respects. If he does not, ask him and assure yourself he carries both.
4. Federal Specifications—If the contractor is selling you cellulose insulation, ask whether the product meets federal specification. The appropriate specification is tagged HHI-515D, and the

contractor should supply evidence of compliance with the specification.
5. UL Labels—If the product you're considering carries an Underwriters' Laboratories label ask whether it is based on a one-time rating or on continuous re-examination. The latter means that the product is checked at random intervals over a long period of time and is much more desirable than a one-time rating.
6. At Installation Time—Arrange with the contractor to show you the materials to be used. Foam products are the exception; for others, you should be assured of the proper quantity and have an opportunity to inspect the material. Don't buy unmarked bags or bundles.
7. Assurance of Workmanship—Rate a contractor very high if he offers a post-installation test. He may arrange for an infrared photograph or use a pistol-shaped heat scanner. These scanners register small temperature differences and will check out a wall in only a few seconds.

# WEATHER-STRIPPING WINDOWS

Installing weather stripping and caulking around doors and windows is probably the least costly, least time consuming, and one of the most effective energy-saving measures you can take in your house.

It has been estimated that about 40 percent of the energy wasted in a typical single-family home is lost through infiltration of air, and an astounding 98 percent of this loss occurs around doors and at windows. These figures clearly demonstrate the importance of having a good, tight fit around all of the openings. To achieve a significantly reduced level of air infiltration, you should consider installing both caulking and weather stripping.

## A Word About Fresh Air

Keep in mind that a certain amount of fresh air infiltration is necessary for your family's health, and for the proper and safe operation of oil- and gas-fired heating equipment.

The National Bureau of Standards suggests that air leakage of about 30 cubic feet per minute should provide the proper fresh air infiltration for a family of four. But to give you an idea of how much leeway that provides most homeowners, consider this fact: A typical home has an infiltration rate of more than 200 cubic feet per minute, or more than six times what is necessary. To determine for sure whether your home requires weather stripping, as most homes do, wait for a windy day and feel around the windows and

doors. If you can feel air coming in between the window or door and the frame, then weather stripping should be a high priority for you.

## Types of Weather Stripping

It seems that there are nearly as many weather-stripping products as there are hardware stores, but most fall into these three basic categories: spring metal, rolled vinyl and felt, and foam rubber.

Part of your decision on which to buy will be based on ease of installation for the type of windows you have. You'll also want to keep in mind how each window operates—one type might be better for your swinging windows and another for sliders.

As you look over each window, measure it and then total up the amounts you'll need of each type. Add about ten percent for waste. It's unwise to skimp and try to get by with too many splices; the effectiveness of the weather stripping depends on a tight squeeze-fit to seal out drafts.

## Installing Spring Metal

To install the spring metal strips (A) in double-hung windows, first move each sash to the open position and cut the weather stripping to fit; avoid covering the pulleys in the upper channels (B). Then carefully align the strips in the appropriate channels, and nail in place. Drive a small nail into each of the holes provided.

After each strip is attached, gently pry up the leaf with a long screwdriver to get the best possible seal (C).

Next, fasten a strip to the bottom surface of the lower sash's bottom rail (D) and to the top surface of the upper sash's top rail. They should compress when the window is shut. Be sure the strips

run the full width of the sash, and it's best if you don't have a splice.

Where the sashes meet, nail a strip to the inside surface of the bottom rail of the upper sash. You may need to flatten the strip to make it fit (E).

On casement windows, tack strips to the frame with the open part facing the inside (F) so the windows will open and close with minimum effort.

## Installing Rolled Vinyl

Vinyl weather stripping (G) has a bulb edge that, when installed properly, compresses slightly to make a tight seal (H). When installing this type of weather stripping, be sure to line it up properly before nailing it in place so that it makes a snug seal, but not so tight as to hamper the movement of the window.

To seal double-hung windows with this type of stripping, attach the strips to the outside of the window (I and J).

Also, seal the joint between the sashes by tacking the strip to the bottom of the upper sash (K). Be careful to cover the joint well.

On awning or casement windows, attach the strips to the outside of the window frame itself (L).

## Installing Foam Rubber

Foam rubber (M) comes in long rolls and is easily pressed into place. Just peel off its protective tape to expose the adhesive side and stick it down as you go. Press the foam rubber to the tops of the upper rails and to the bottoms of the lower rails of your double-hung windows (N).

Foam rubber is usually best for metal casement or tilt-out windows. Install it on all four sides of the frame, where the window unit touches (O).

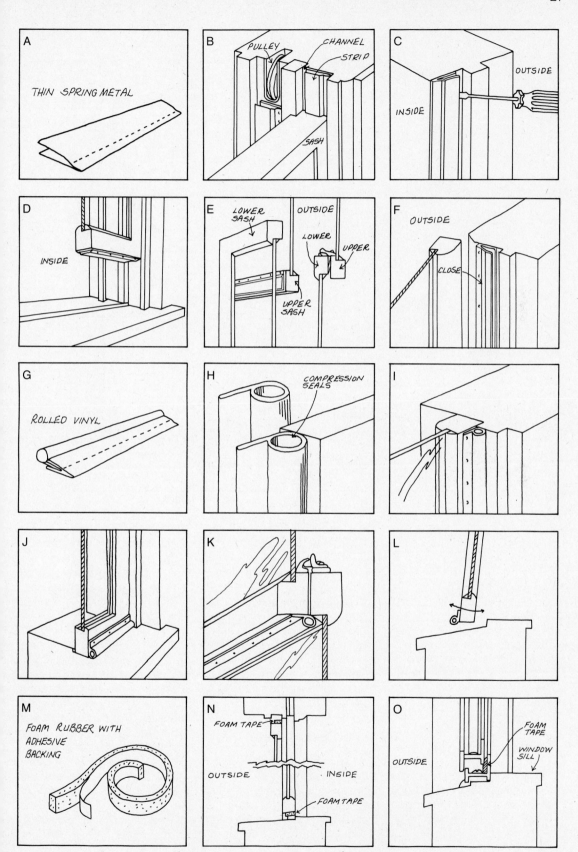

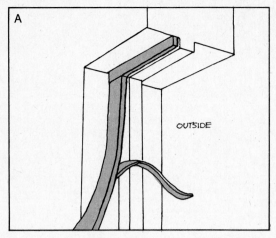

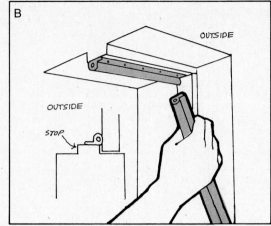

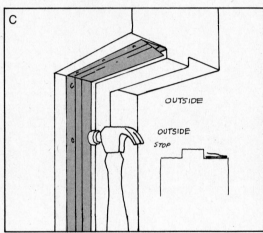

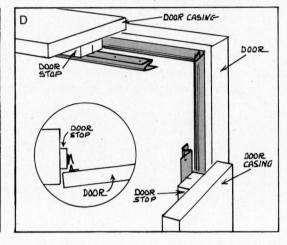

# WEATHER-STRIPPING DOORS

There is a vast array of weather stripping for doors. Some such as adhesive-backed foam can be used all around a door frame. Others are for specific parts of a door, such as the sides and the top or the bottom edge.

## Foam Rubber

This is the easiest of the door weather strippings to install. All you need to do is cut it to the appropriate length, peel the backing off the adhesive, and press in place on the insides of the stops (A).

## Rolled Vinyl

This is the same type used for windows. It has a bulb that, when properly installed, compresses slightly to make a tight seal. Tack this type to the face of the door stops. Be sure to align the strips so the bulb edges fit snugly against the door (B).

## Spring Metal

Nail spring metal strips to the jamb, inside the stop (C). With this type you'll need to allow for the latch and lock. Also, once the stripping is in place, lift the outer edge of the strip with a screwdriver to provide a tight seal.

## Interlocking Metal Channels

Interlocking metal channels form a good seal, but are tricky to install. Nail to both the outside face of the door and the stop (D). A disadvantage of these channels is that they are exposed to the elements, which could cause deterioration of the metal. There is another type of metal channel, known as J-Strips, that is not visible after installation. Because J-Strips are out of the way they are not subject to exposure damage. The problem with these strips is that they require a notch be cut in

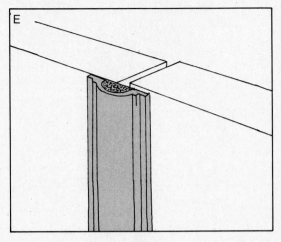

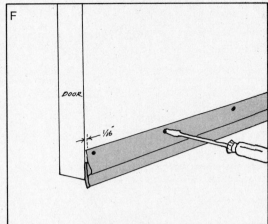

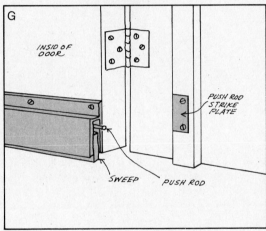

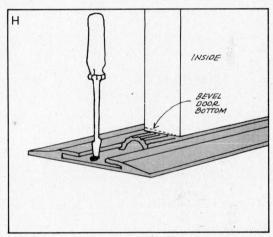

both the door and the frame. This should not be attempted by anyone but a most accomplished handyman. If you don't consider yourself in this category, such an installation is best left to a professional carpenter.

## Insulated Molding

Use this specially designed molding to seal the gap between double doors. Nail to the face of the door that is usually closed (E).

## Door Thresholds

In addition to the weather stripping mentioned above, there are other types designed just for weather stripping thresholds.

The easiest of these to install is a sweep (F). Simply attach it to the bottom of the door. Some are designed for inside application, others for outside. Examine your threshold and door bottom to decide which would be a more practical application for your door, and select a sweep accordingly. If your door opens in, as do most entry doors, the inside sweep probably will be better for you. When installing, cut it slightly in from the edges of the door.

A somewhat more complex version of the sweep is the pop-up type that rises when the door is opened and lowers automatically when the door is closed. This allows the sweep to clear carpeting as the door

opens. Fit this type flush with the door bottom and attach it to the inside surface with screws. Next, position the push rod strike plate (G) and mark the spot. Chisel a recess for the plate and attach it flush with the door jamb.

Another alternative is a door "shoe," which can be installed on the floor or threshold instead of the door (H). You'll need to remove the door. Then cut the shoe to fit the opening exactly. Remove vinyl strip to screw the "shoe" in place, then snap the vinyl back in the groove. Cut the bottom of the door for an exact fit. Use a portable circular saw and bevel the cut slightly. Get a snug fit—but not so tight that the door won't open easily. Then, rehang the door.

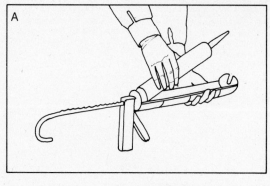

# CAULKING YOUR HOME

Caulking is easy to do, and is an effective way of preventing air or water infiltration. Caulking should be applied wherever there are joints in the exterior wall of your home. This includes around the frames of windows and doors, at corners where the siding joins, along the top of the foundation where the wood frame meets masonry, and where pipes and wires enter.

The best tool for applying caulking is an inexpensive half-barrel gun (A). Standard caulking cartridges drop right into the gun.

## Caulking Products

Caulk falls into three broad categories: traditional oil- or resin-based compounds, rubber-derived formulations such as latex and butyl, and synthetic-based materials. The type you select depends largely upon the job you want it to do and the amount you need.

Before buying any type, read its data to learn about surface preparation, what materials the caulk will adhere to, and how long it must cure before you can paint over it. Here's a list of the most commonly available products, ranked from least to most costly:

*Oil-base:* Although it bonds to most surfaces if they're clean and dry, oil-base caulk is falling into disfavor. Now there are better products available.

*Latex:* A good general-purpose sealant that is fast-drying, latex is ideal for filling small cracks and joints, patching plaster walls. It can be painted.

*Butyl:* This is exceptionally good for sealing seams in gutters and joints between metal and masonry and for filling wide cracks. After curing it remains flexible, but can be painted.

*Vinyl:* Highly adhesive as well as waterproof and weatherproof, this type is excellent for use around wet areas such as tubs and showers.

*Silicone:* Save this type for small jobs where exceptional adhesion and long-lasting elasticity are necessary. It is great for sealing around tubs, showers, outdoor outlets, and fixtures. However, it is expensive and paint won't adhere to it as well as to most.

## Applying Caulking

Before applying caulking, first scrape the area to be caulked to remove dirt, peeling paint, and deteriorated caulking (B).

Next, you will have to cut the tip of the nozzle on the caulking cartridge. The nozzle is narrow at the tip and widens as it goes down. Determine how wide a bead you will need for your job, and cut the nozzle appropriately, with a slight angle.

When applying the caulking hold the gun at an angle and move in a direction away from the flow of the caulking (C).

Make sure the bead is wide enough to cover both of the adjoining surfaces between which you are caulking. Getting the bead to flow evenly and neatly takes a little practice, so when you begin, carry a wet rag with you to wipe up your mistakes.

Some caulking material comes in a rope form and can be shoved into crevices with your fingers (D). Some of this type of caulking retains its flexibility and can be removed when desired just by pulling it off.

# STORM WINDOWS AND DOORS

Doors and windows—we need them, and can't live without them. But if we could, our home's energy consumption would drop noticeably because windows and doors as a group provide the greatest single energy drain on a home. After all, doors and windows literally are materials used to plug holes in the wall. The quality and fit of the windows and doors obviously play important roles in determining how much heat leaks in and out of your home. And, these leaks are what the heating equipment must work to overcome.

## Heat Escape Trio

Scientists tell us that there are three ways windows and doors rob us of energy. One is the infiltration of air through leaks around doors and windows. Another is the conductance of heat through a material such as glass. The final culprit is radiation. This is the transmission of solar energy into a building.

Infiltration hits us year-round—in both heating and cooling seasons. Conductance rears its ugly head primarily during the heating season, and radiation gets us in the summertime when solar heat gain is unwanted.

## Fighting Back

Fortunately, there are several ways for the wise homeowner to strike back at this trio. Weather stripping and caulking (see pages 20 to 24) are two ways. Another very important and potent weapon is the installation of storm windows and doors.

## Storm Windows

If you had to choose between installing storm windows or installing storm doors, you should install the windows. As a rule, they save more energy than do storm doors, although it is by far best to install both.

It is important to have the double glazing provided by storm windows because of the very poor thermal qualities of glass. Indeed, as far as insulating properties of glass are concerned, a single pane of it provides almost no resistance. However, when you double glaze by putting up a storm window you make the glass area of that window twice as resistant to conduction losses during the winter. At the same time, the additional frame of the storm window helps slash infiltration around the prime window. The air between the storm and prime windows also becomes an important additional insulator, and last, but not least, storm windows even help during the summer cooling season by reducing solar transmission by about 10 to 15 percent.

An added benefit is that the storm windows help keep the inside glass surface warm during the wintertime, which helps prevent condensation and ice formation on the glass.

But what if you already have insulated glass in your primary windows? Should you still have a storm window? The answer depends largely on where you live. If you live in a part of the country where the thermometer really dips during the winter, then storm windows still would be beneficial. This is especially so for windows facing north since they are exposed to the prevailing winter winds.

## Buying Storm Windows and Doors

Once you have decided to invest in storm windows and doors, you must decide whether you want to do the job yourself, or have a contractor do the work for you.

Making sure windows and doors are square, level, and plumb when they are installed is tricky, and should not be tackled by the inexperienced do-it-yourselfer. In addition, mistakes in measuring can be costly and you may find yourself paying for windows or doors that don't fit. But doing it yourself is not impossible and you may find the savings worth it. Get complete, detailed advice from your supplier on how to measure for the type of window you want. Then measure each window twice to be sure you'll get windows that fit.

If you hire a contractor, he will be responsible for the whole job. Check his workmanship carefully because poor construction or sloppy installation of storm windows and doors can seriously impair their effectiveness.

And before you pay the contractor for the finished work, make sure the windows and doors fit tightly and operate smoothly.

# PROJECTS YOU CAN BUILD

We hope that after looking at the projects in this section, you'll turn back to one of your favorites and say, "I'm going to build this one!" After all, that's why we've included the section. But don't assume that this need be your only energy-saving tac- tic—or your first. These projects are merely frosting on the cake. So if you haven't plugged all the energy leaks around your house yet or taken advantage of the other hints in this book, start there first and build your project later.

# VENETIAN BLIND BUMP-OUT

Keeping the inside of your home cool during the summer is becoming an ever-more-expensive task. And with utility rates constantly on the rise, you won't get any relief there. So your job is to make sure your air conditioner doesn't run more often than necessary. One way to do this is to search out windows that magnify the sun's rays at crucial times of the day and repel the warming force. This truly attractive venetian blind assembly works outside where heat-gain troubles begin.

**1** Start by examining the frame around the outside of the window to see whether there is adequate surface available to attach the boxlike venetian blind enclosure. If there isn't, you'll have to anchor it directly to the sidewalls of the house. Also check to see whether the window frame is in good condition, with caulking around the edges, and whether the glazing compound holding the window panes in place is intact. If not, now's the time to make needed repairs.

**2** Tailor the size of the project to fit snugly around the window you'll be framing. When doing your figuring, don't worry about whether you'll be able to purchase a venetian blind to fit the space. Many widths and several lengths are available. And when deciding on materials, you should consider using redwood, cedar, or pressure-treated wood, as each of these woods will stand up well to the weather. If you select another type of wood, remember that you'll have to treat it with a penetrating stain/sealer or exterior paint later on to protect against the damaging effects of moisture.

**3** Begin constructon by cutting two 1x8s (A) for the sides of the enclosure. Notch them at the top to accommodate a 1x4 facing strip to be applied later (see sketch). Screw both sides securely to the window frame, or, if necessary, attach them to the sidewall of the house with metal angles and screws. If you're dealing with a brick or other hard surface, attach the metal angles with screws driven into expansion anchors. You'll find mortar joints the easiest place to drill holes for the anchors.

**4** Rip ¾ inch off the width of a 1x8 to form the top of the enclosure (B). Use screws and glue to attach enclosure top to the sides (A) as well as to the top of the window frame.

**5** Cut the 1x8 bottom board (C) to size, and attach it beneath the sill of the window and to the sides as shown. Here again, use screws and glue.

**6** Complete construction of the boxlike frame by adding a 1x4 trim strip (D).

**7** Fasten a metal channel (E) to the inside of each side of the box, recessing each approximately ¾ inch from the outside edge of the frame.

**8** Mount a venetian blind to the underside of the unit's top so that when you lower it the edges will fall into the metal channels along the sides. (This will keep the blind from swinging against the window when the wind blows.) Note: An aluminum or a steel blind with a baked-on enamel finish is probably the best product for this particular situation. Either will stand up well to the weather.

**9** Complete the project by caulking around the edges of the frame and painting or staining the unit, if necessary or desired.

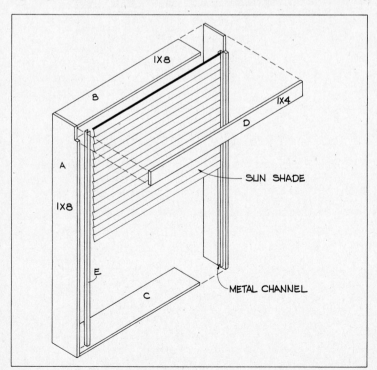

# HOME-GROWN SUNSHIELD

**This decorator trellis can be a striking accent to your landscaping plan ... and an unexpected energy saver. It serves both functions beautifully when covered with leafy greenery.**

**1** The simple design of this project makes it easy to adapt to any width or height. If you position the structure on the west side of your home, which is where it will do the most good, you'll want it tall enough to turn back that blazing, late-afternoon summer sun. Several factors will affect the needed height of the trellis, most notably the amount of overhang your home has and the latitude of your area. When you've determined the size and location of the trellis, stake out the spots for the posts.

**2** Dig 8-inch-diameter postholes deep enough to extend below the frost line. (Check with a builder; he'll know how deep the frost line is in your area.)

**3** Miter the tops of the two 2x4 uprights (A). Because the trellis must face up to the rigors of weather changes, it's best to use redwood, cedar, or pressure-treated wood. But if you use another type of wood, soak or brush the bottoms of the uprights with "penta" (pentachlorophenol). Also apply the penta to any portion of the uprights that will come within six inches or so of grade. Allow them to dry about two days.

**4** Toss some gravel or rocks into the holes, then set the uprights in concrete, making sure they are plumb. Use enough concrete so that it extends slightly above ground. As it sets, shape the concrete to ensure adequate drainage. Allow the concrete to cure for at least one week.

**5** Miter the 2x4 top plate (B) and secure it in place, using galvanized nails. Also fasten metal angles at the joints for extra strength.

**6** Connect the uprights at the bottom by toenailing a 2x4 stretcher (C) into place and reinforcing it with metal angles.

**7** Attach a piece of light-gauge welded wire fencing (D) to the frame, using sturdy staples. (If your local building supply center doesn't carry the large mesh fencing, try a farm supply outlet.)

**8** If you've used redwood, cedar, or pressure-treated wood for the fence frame, paint it, stain it, treat it with weathering oil, or let it weather naturally. If you've opted for another type wood, prime the wood, then give it two coats of oil-base paint.

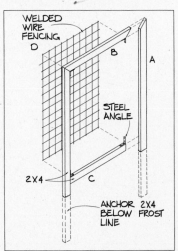

WELDED WIRE FENCING D

B

A

STEEL ANGLE

2X4

C

ANCHOR 2X4 BELOW FROST LINE

# AWNING-TYPE SUNSHADE

Not so many years ago, people used awnings of one type or another to shade windows because they helped keep the house cool. Today, awnings are enjoying renewed popularity for much the same reason—they help cut air-conditioning costs. The awning shown here is as effective as the old-fashioned kind and a lot more stylish. Easy too!

**1** This project adapts easily to almost any size window. Make the awning material the same width as the window trim. Use canvas or nylon for the awning.
**2** Sew a loop at one end of the material (A) to accommodate a section of 1-inch-diameter pipe.
**3** To the back side of the material's other end sew a 2-inch-wide Velcro strip (B). Attach a second Velcro strip above the window frame using staples or nails.
**4** Buy 1-inch galvanized pipe cut to size—and threaded where necessary—to form the frame of the awning. Insert one section of pipe (C) through the loop in the awning material. Screw on an elbow (D) at each end.
**5** Attach awning supports (E) to the elbows.
**6** Attach flagpole brackets (F) to your home's sidewalls.
**7** Hang the awning by pressing the Velcro strips together and inserting the pipe supports (E) into the flagpole brackets.

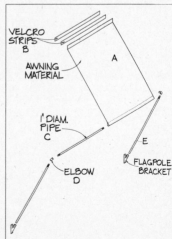

# SCULPTURED SPLIT-LEVEL DECK

**Here's proof that an energy-saving project can add beauty to your home as well as be functional. This spectacular deck provides privacy, plus protection from the sun and wind. And it's adaptable to just about any situation or terrain. The deck shown here faces west—notice the sun-screening canopy and louvered front panel for extra afternoon comfort. On page 33, you'll see how to modify the design for east or south exposures.**

**1** Decide how large you want your deck to be. A good rule of thumb is to figure 20 square feet each for the maximum number of people you'll likely have on the deck at one time. Then, check local zoning regulations—there may be "set-back" restrictions requiring you to place the structure a certain distance away from property lines. Also, you should be sure where your lot lines are, check the property deed for easements that might influence construction, and determine the location of underground utilities. The local utilities have this information.

When choosing materials for your deck, be aware of local building codes (especially in snowy climates where roof supports need to be strong enough to handle heavy snow loads). To ensure long-lasting good looks, select pressure-treated lumber, redwood, or cedar for your deck.
**2** Plan both levels of the deck carefully, noting any change in elevation of the terrain. You'll find putting your plan on graph paper

will help at this stage and also when you order materials later.

**3** Stake the location of the corner posts. To do this, first drive stakes next to the house at the desired locations. Then stretch string or mason's line perpendicular to the house and drive stakes the appropriate distance out. Square up the corners, readjusting stakes if necessary. If the size of your deck makes intermediate posts necessary, stake their locations, too.

**4** Cut away strips of sod to prepare the site for the deck.

**5** Using a posthole digger or auger, dig holes for the posts (A). Dig the holes deep enough so the posts will extend below the frost line when set.

**6** Spread sheets of dark-colored polyethylene film over the excavated site and cover with bark, pebbles, or crushed stone to prevent weed growth.

**7** Set posts for the deck. If you pour concrete footings for the posts, use forms above ground to shape the concrete. Also, be sure to imbed connecting hardware in the concrete. Machine and carriage bolts both work well for this purpose.

To set posts directly into concrete, first line the bottom of the holes with a few inches of rocks. Then set the posts, plumb them, and nail up outrigger stakes to steady the posts. Fill the holes with concrete, mounding it slightly above the surface. Allow the concrete to cure at least one week. (If you use pressure-treated lumber, you can set the posts directly into the ground.)

**8** Determine the height you want the canopy beams to be, then

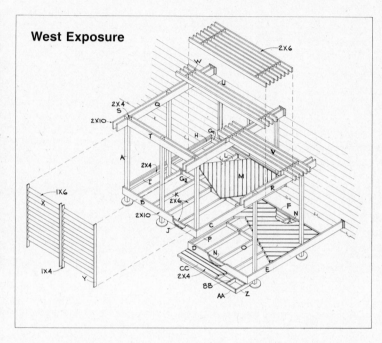

**West Exposure**

stretch a mason's line from the house to the corner posts. Hang a line level from the line to ensure level cutoff marks. Cut perimeter posts the same height.

**9** Determine the deck surface heights and stretch a mason's line as before, marking these heights on the appropriate posts. Then cut any intermediate post to the appropriate height. Don't forget to subtract the thickness of the decking material.

**10** Frame around the posts for the upper level of the deck with 2x10s (B,C), mitering the corners and positioning the top of each flush with the desired floor height. Bolt the 2x10s to the posts, and secure them to the house with joist hangers. Repeat the procedure to

frame around the lower level of the deck with 2x10s (D,E,F).

**11** Using lag screws, fasten a 2x6 nailer (G-1) to the house as shown, recessing it the thickness of the decking material.

**12** Provide additional support by nailing a 2x6 stretcher (G-2) between the frame's side members.

**13** Install 2x4 ledgers (H,I) and 2x6 ledgers (J) along the inside of the 2x10 framing as shown. Then, form a grid, using 2x6 joists (K,L). Nail the joists in place or use joist hangers.

**14** Nail 2x6 decking (M) to the joists in the pattern you desire. Trim around posts.

**15** Repeat framing procedures for the lower deck, using 2x6 members (N,O) and 2x4 mem-

## East Exposure

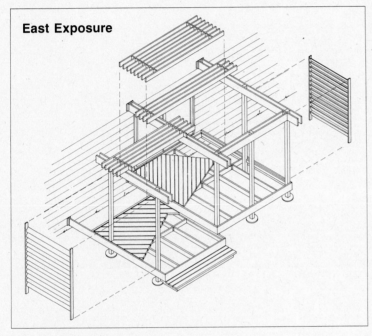

## South Exposure

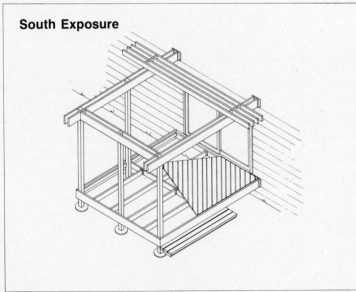

bers (P). Nail decking to the framework.

**16** Using carriage bolts, attach beams (Q,R) to the uprights. Use joists hangers to attach (Q) to the house.

**17** Attach short 2x4 wood cleats (S) as shown to the outside corner posts of the upper level deck. Bolt cross beams (T) to the cleats and the 4x4 post.

**18** Toenail 2x6 canopy members (U,V) to the beams, alternating with short 2x6 spacers (W). Use as many members as needed to protect your deck from the sun.

**19** Butt 1x6 louvers (X) between 1x4 verticals (Y) to form the front screen assemblies. Nail the screens between deck posts as shown.

**20** For the step support, construct a box made from pressure-treated 2x4s (Z,AA,BB). Notch Z to fit around the concrete footing and bolt to the inside of the 4x4 posts. Space members BB at 12- to 16-inch intervals for adequate support of tread. Attach 2x4 treads (CC) to top of box support.

### East Exposure

Follow the same basic procedures described previously. Add louvered panels at either end of the assembly as shown to block harsh winds and sun.

### South Exposure

Construct only the upper level of the deck as described. Install just enough canopy slats to provide protection from the sun. Position the step up to the deck at the side of the structure as shown.

# FLOWERY
# SUN
# SHIELD

**There's nothing like a sunny south or west window exposure for highlighting a display of your showiest flowers. Those same windows, though, let the hot sun stream in, which can play havoc with summertime cooling bills. Rather than shutting off your view with heavy draperies or shades, take the heat off with this attractive flower box with translucent lid.**

**1** Though the project shown here adorns a fairly small window, you can rescale it to fit much larger windows as well. Make the unit somewhat taller than the window you're shielding and wide enough to clear the window trim and sill. **2** Since redwood, cedar, and pressure-treated wood weather well, it's a good idea to build the entire unit with one of these materials. If you use any other wood, be sure to finish the project by painting with a good exterior paint or applying a penetrating stain and sealer.

**3** Assemble the flower box from ¾-inch exterior plywood. Butt the sides (A,B) together, and attach the bottom (C) using screws and glue. Drill ½-inch holes in the bottom to facilitate drainage, and treat the inside of the box liberally with penta (pentachlorophenol) to keep it from rotting. Set aside to dry for at least two days.

**4** Frame window top and sides with 1x2 strips (D,E) screwed directly into the wall studs. After the flower box dries, attach it with screws to the wall studs just below the sill.

**5** Cut six lengths of 1x6 boards (F) to fit, trimming the tops at a 30° angle. Butt the boards together (or leave slight spaces between each, if desired) and screw them to the flower box. Brace the siding at the top with 1x2 ledgers (G), cut to fit and attached flush with the top inside edge of the siding boards.

**6** Have a piece of ⅛-inch translucent acrylic plastic of the appropriate dimensions formed to match the shape shown (see sketch). (Check the yellow pages under "Plastics" to locate a supplier.) Drill holes through the plastic sheet and screw it into the top of the 1x6 boards (F), bedding it wherever necessary in caulk for a weathertight seal. (Note: Before drilling holes in acrylic, secure the material so it won't move around. Also, back the plastic with a wood scrap to prevent it from chipping when the drill penetrates the plastic's backside.)

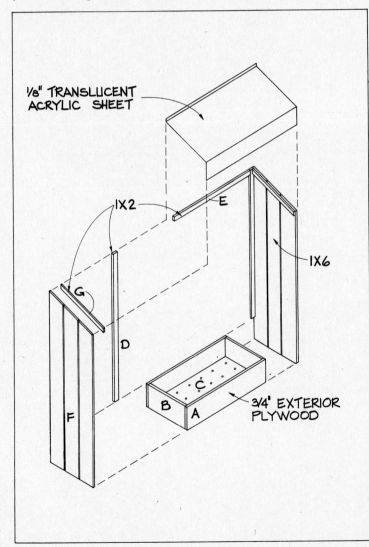

⅛" TRANSLUCENT ACRYLIC SHEET

1X2

E

G

1X6

D

F

B  C  A

¾' EXTERIOR PLYWOOD

## SHADY CANVAS CANOPY

A leisurely day on a patio or deck is a summer treat everyone loves—but not when too much sun is scorching down. Red-hot days are tough on air conditioner costs, too, and that's why this canopy is such a bargain. It shades an exposed set of windows while it protects the patio. Plus ... it's easy up, easy down for hassle-free winter storage.

**1** In planning this project, keep in mind that it should not extend farther than about 30 inches beyond your roof's overhang. Otherwise, you'll have trouble with too much downward pressure, which will cause the unit to sag or to come apart.

**2** Cut 2x4 and 1x4 frame members (A,B) to the desired lengths.

**3** Before assembling the frame, drill ¾-inch holes in the 1x4s. Space the holes so as to provide adequate support for the canvas.

**4** Assemble the frame, using glue and screws. Use butt joints.

**5** Measure the distance between your home's siding and the inside edge of the fascia board. Cut 1x2 soffit fillers (C) to fit that space and attach them to the frame with glue and screws. Paint or stain the unit as desired.

**6** Using a hacksaw, cut several lengths of ¾-inch aluminum tubing about one inch longer than the depth of the frame. Insert the "dowels" (D) through the holes in the frame. If desired, paint the metal with aluminized paint.

**7** Buy a strip of heavy canvas that's six inches longer and two or three inches narrower than the frame. Finish the ends by folding the canvas over (about one inch), stitching the seams shut, and affixing grommets every six inches. Weave the canvas through the dowels in the frame. Screw the canvas into the bottom of each end of the frame.

**8** Lift the canopy into position. Secure it by driving lag screws through the back of the frame into your home's sidewalls. Provide more support by fastening metal straps as shown in the detail.

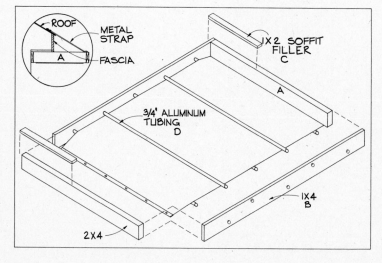

# EYEBROW EAVE EXTENSION

**Energy-saving projects needn't be strictly functional. Far from it! Here's one that will deflect the summer heat away from your window in fine fashion— yet it's a dramatic departure from the traditional awning. Use several of these stylish sunscreens around your home to add a whole new architectural flair to the lines of your roof.**

**1** This project, though not difficult to construct, does require you to cut some of the members at an angle that matches the pitch of your roof. Also, keep in mind that the project is best suited to shade narrow windows. Making the unit too wide can result in support problems.

**2** Construct the 1x6 frame (A,B,C) as shown in the sketch. You'll want the frame to extend back under the soffit and butt up against the house. Use screws and glue at all joints.

**3** Nail 2x2s (D) to the frame, spacing them evenly to form a lattice-like appearance. Wait till later to nail up the four 2x2s nearer to the house.

**4** Face the frame with a 1x10 (E) whose bottom edge is flush with the bottom of the 2x2s. Bevel its top edge.

**5** Measure the distance from the inside of the fascia board to the siding. Cut 1x1 soffit fillers (F) to fit, then nail them to the 1x6 frame as shown. Paint or stain the frame as desired.

**6** Construct the louver (G,H,I). Bevel the members so they match the pitch of the roof, then notch as shown. You'll want to make the louver deep enough that it fills the space between the gutter and the 1x10 facer (see detail). Glue and nail the members together. Paint or stain the louver to match the frame. Nail to the frame.

**7** With a helper, lift the unit into place. Secure it to the house by driving lag screws through the frame's back piece. Add more support by screwing metal straps to both the unit and the roof.

**8** Nail up the last four 2x2 slats.

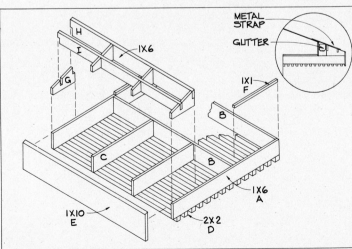

# SLIDING DOOR WIND AND SUN SHELTER

**When it comes to keeping things cool in the summer and warm in the winter, sliding glass doors aren't exactly man's best friend. However, you can help to make yours a little more practical (and a lot nicer to look at!) with a sleek enclosure like the one here.**

**1** In planning this project, keep in mind that in order for the structure to succeed as a natural extension of your home, you must select materials that harmonize with or complement those used on the house itself. You'll want the roofline to be in keeping with the house, too.

**2** Assemble the frames for the sidewalls first, building them flat on the ground for easier construction. Nail the uprights (A) and crosspieces (B,C) together as shown in the sketch.

**3** Frame the sliding door opening with three 2x4s (D,E), nailing each to the wall studs.

**4** Nail the previously constructed sidewall frames to the 2x4s surrounding the sliding glass door. Toenail a 2x4 top plate (F) to connect the sidewalls; then, strengthen the construction by nailing two crosspieces (G) into place.

**5** Locate the vertical wall studs above the sliding door and attach a 2x4 nailer (H) to the house. Position the 2x4 nailer high enough to give you the slope you want for the roof.

**6** Beveling ends whenever necessary, toenail short 2x4 "rafters" (I,J) into place.

**7** Cut sheets of ⅝-inch exterior plywood siding (K) to cover the sidewalls. Secure the panels to the frame, using galvanized nails.

**8** Line the inside of the enclosure's frame with ⅜-inch exterior plywood (L,M). Add 1x6 trim strips ripped and cut to fit (N,O) to finish off the front of the unit.

**9** Cut a piece of ⅜-inch exterior plywood (P) to serve as underlayment for the shingles. Nail on the roof sheathing and cover it with building paper. Then nail a strip of metal drip edge to the bottom of the sheathing.

**10** Cover the roof with cedar shingles or with a type and color that harmonize with the shingles on your house. Overlap the edges of the roof with the shingles.

**11** Nail some flashing at the point where the roof of the enclosure meets the house. Seal the flashing with roofing tar.

**12** Paint or stain the unit an appropriate color. If you use stain, choose one designed to penetrate and seal the wood. Caulk around the base of the unit.

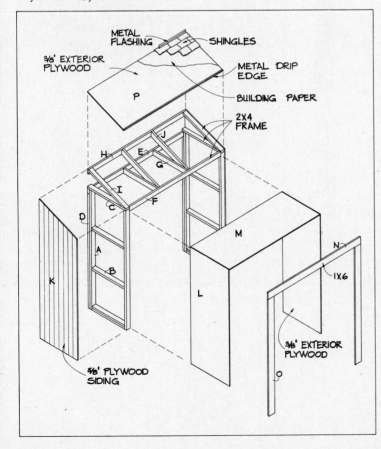

METAL FLASHING

SHINGLES

⅜' EXTERIOR PLYWOOD

METAL DRIP EDGE

BUILDING PAPER

2X4 FRAME

P

J

H   E   G

I

C   F

D

A

B

M

N

K

L

1X6

⅜" EXTERIOR PLYWOOD

O

⅝' PLYWOOD SIDING

# PANELIZED INTERIOR VESTIBULE

**Having a vestibule leading into your home is no small blessing these days. In addition to providing a place for family and friends to shed their wraps, vestibules create an air-lock situation that helps keep unconditioned air from penetrating the rest of the house. That means more money in your pocket because of lower utility bills. This interior vestibule does its job . . . with style.**

**1** When planning this project, keep in mind that you want to achieve a snug fit top to bottom and side to side. So take care that your dimensions are extremely accurate. Note: Make the panels a bit shorter than the ceiling height. Otherwise, positioning them will be difficult. Also, in terms of materials, you should use 2x2 finish-grade stock for the frame and tempered hardboard for the panel inserts. For the upper panel inserts, you may want to substitute acrylic sheet for the hardboard.

**2** For each large stationary panel (there are four of them), cut the outer frame members (A,B). Miter the corners as shown in the sketch. Using a table saw or a router, cut a ½-inch-deep dado ¼ inch with to accommodate the hardboard panels to be inserted later. Glue and nail three sides of the outer frame together.

**3** Cut two crosspieces (C) to serve as dividers between the upper and the lower panels. Cut a dado in each as described in step 2, and attach the crosspieces to the three-sided frame.

**4** Carefully slide the ¼-inch hardboard panels (D,E) into the frame's grooves.

**5** Secure the fourth side of the frame with glue and nails to complete the panel assembly.

**6** Assemble each large stationary panel as described in steps 2 through 5.

**7** For the smaller stationary panels, join the framing members (F,G) as before, using either hardboard or acrylic sheet for the panels (E).

**8** Assemble the movable panels (H,I) as before.

**9** Paint the frame and panels. Or, if desired, cover the panel inserts with fabric, wallpaper, or similar material.

**10** Position the outermost panels and secure them by driving screws through the frame into the ceiling and floor. Set subsequent panels at the desired angle and secure them the same way. Fill the small gap created by the angle with a filler strip of scrap lumber or a piece of quarter round (J). This is a two-person job, as the panels need to be steadied while the strips are being nailed.

**11** Finish the zigzag vestibule wall by hanging the door panels using butt hinges. To minimize the gap between the door and stationary panels, recess the hinges.

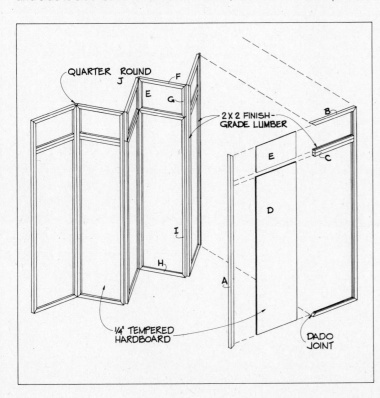

QUARTER ROUND J

2 X 2 FINISH-GRADE LUMBER

¼" TEMPERED HARDBOARD

DADO JOINT

# TAILOR-MADE INTERIOR VESTIBULE

Many vestibules serve only as air locks—barriers between the interior of a house and the elements outside. However, this vestibule does more. Besides saving you energy, it provides much-needed shelving and adds architectural interest to both your entryway and your living room.

**1** Before constructing this project, carefully plan the layout. Shown at left is a fairly standard arrangement, but it may not work for your entry situation. If it won't, turn to pages 44 and 45 for other adaptations of this same idea. One of them should work well for your layout.

**2** Begin by determining which way your ceiling's joists run, then nail the vestibule's top plates (A,B,C) to the joists in the desired location.

**3** If there's carpeting in the area where the vestibule will be, pull the carpeting and pad up and move them back out of the way.

**4** Using a line and plumb bob, mark the location of the soleplates (D,E,F). Then cut the plates to size and nail them to the floor.

**5** Double-check the positioning of the top and soleplates to make sure that they align exactly. Any mistakes made in aligning the two elements will haunt you in the later stages of the project.

**6** Using the framing plan shown in the sketch, toenail studs (G) between the top and soleplates.

**7** Toenail the door header members (H) into place. Do the same for the shelf and bookcase cavity headers (I,J). Support double header (I) with 2x4 studs (K) as shown in detail. Complete the framework by nailing members L,M into place.

**8** Frame the bookshelf divider by butting 2x4s (N,O) as shown in the sketch. Secure the members to each other with metal angles. Center the frame in the opening that will house the bookshelves and secure it to the surrounding framing and floor.

**9** Prepare the opening for the pre-hung door by removing part of the soleplate (dotted lines); then position the door and secure it to the framing.

**10** If you plan to run any wiring to the vestibule, do so now; run the electrical wiring through the studs and plates.

**11** Cover the framing members with drywall. Tape and texture the drywall. (You may want to have a professional come in and do this part of the project for you because finishing drywall is a skill that takes time to master. Even professionals admit this.)

**12** Screw the adjustable shelf supports to the framing as shown in the sketch. Cut the plywood shelves (P) to size. Finish them as desired, making sure to fill the edges of the shelves. Then position them as desired on clips attached to the supports.

**13** Cut door trim (Q,R) to fit; finish it as desired and nail it in position.

**14** If desired, add molding above the shelving.

**15** Install a threshold, and cut off the door so as to achieve a snug fit at the bottom.

**16** Replace the carpeting so that it fits flush against the vestibule or adapt the floor covering idea in the example shown here.

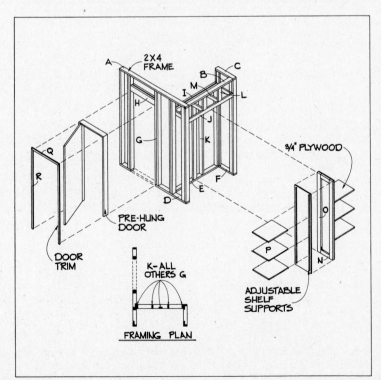

2X4 FRAME

¾" PLYWOOD

PRE-HUNG DOOR

DOOR TRIM

K-ALL OTHERS G

FRAMING PLAN

ADJUSTABLE SHELF SUPPORTS

# VESTIBULE OPTIONS

Your own front entry situation plays a big part in how you choose to create an interior vestibule air lock. The project on the previous pages will fit many houses, but not all. Here are some alternatives. Chances are one of them will work for you. Just adapt the construction we've shown and you'll get a serviceable air lock that will save energy year-round.

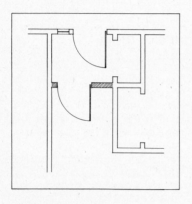 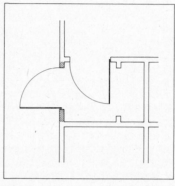 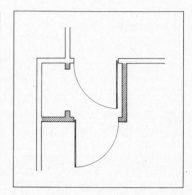

In many houses with a center entry hall, you can create a vestibule as shown in the floor plan above. Here the existing coat closet is in a very typical location and the door at the top of the drawing is the primary door to the outside. Plan the second door wherever it's convenient for your situation. Allow a minimum of 36 inches between the old and new doors—even more space if you are able to. One rule of thumb is to place the doors the same distance apart as the width of the hall.

For help with constructing the wall (shown with hash marks), refer to the sketch on page 43. You'll want to adjust the dimensions to the width of your hallway, of course, and use double 2x4s against each wall. Choose a prehung interior door to make the installation easier. You can plan the door to swing whichever way is more convenient. The arrangement shown works well for traffic going in or out. But you may want to have the door swing into the vestibule if it would interfere with traffic inside the house.

Many L-shaped houses have an existing foyer that can be converted into a vestibule with a minimum of effort. If you're lucky enough to have a situation like the one shown here (the outside door is again at the top of the drawing), you're already halfway to an energy-saving vestibule.

Construction need only consist of a stud wall on each side of the existing entry, a header above the spot for the new door, and the installation of a new pre-hung door. You can extract the stud and header work you need from the exploded view drawing on the previous page. Most likely, you won't need to change any electrical switches.

In a situation such as this, you should plan the swing of the new door so that it opens away from the new vestibule area. This eliminates any potential hassle that the two doors will bump each other. In addition, family members and guests won't have to be inconvenienced by dodging a door each time they enter or leave the house.

This variation is very similar to the solution shown on pages 42-43; the main difference is that you can create a coat closet within the new vestibule where none existed before.

You'll need to follow the same basic steps as those on pages 42-43, starting with the carpeting. Then plan out the new stud walls as indicated by the hash marks in this sketch. Build the new walls with soleplates, 2x4 studs, and top plates as outlined, then add the new door.

You'll need to plan the dimensions carefully; the vestibule itself should not be less than three feet wide. The depth of the closet may be dictated by the space you have available—but you can tailor its width (shown here from top of illustration to bottom) according to how much space you need to hang coats.

In a case such as this, you may need to enlist professional help for changes in your electrical setup. You may have to relocate existing switches to the living room and exterior lights.

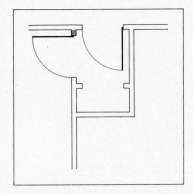 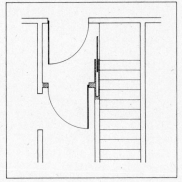 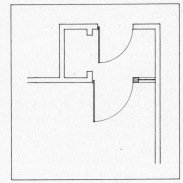

Quite comparable to our second alternative, this existing entry offers an easy way to create an air lock. Again, the outdoors is at the top of the drawing.

All you need to do with a situation such as this is add the short stub wall in the position shown. Next, install a header above the opening for the new door and nail in a pre-hung door unit.

In most houses, plan the new door to swing back out of the way as shown here for the most convenience. But study the opposite swing also, especially if you can avoid moving light switches or if you have an unusual furniture arrangement and traffic route.

This plan also has some other extra advantages. It gives you a built-in opportunity for a new floor covering in the entry that will help take some of the wear and tear off the living room carpeting. And you may want to consider a very plain, ceiling-high door that can be painted to blend with the living room. This way, it will be much less obtrusive when you want to leave it open.

If your house is a two-story, with a stair joining the entry, the problem of adding a vestibule may be especially difficult.

This is one solution that will help you with your situation. In most cases like this, building the air lock also means building in some inconvenience because it's often necessary to open one door to the unheated space, go through and open another to the stairway.

In this instance, a short open railing was removed and a pocket door unit was installed in the space. When closed, the pocket door seals off the second floor.

The other part of the air lock is much the same as our first alternative—all you need to do is construct the two short walls and a header between them, and install a standard door.

A solution such as this will go a long way in saving energy, but you should balance the savings with your family's life-style. If you have small children or are up and down the stairs many times a day, other projects may not create as much inconvenience.

An entry housed in a "sentry box" as illustrated by this plan is ideal for creating a buffer area from the outside. In fact, that was the original purpose in early houses with such a projecting entry.

Here the new, short wall serves as a frame for a single pane of glass. The new door not only helps block the outdoor air from the house, but also helps to create a more defined, formalized entry that didn't exist before.

The construction follows the same pattern as the other alternatives, except that you merely leave an opening for the glass, much as you do for the installation of the new door. The header above the door continues all the way across the existing opening.

The use of a tall pane of glass as shown here is often a good idea in other schemes, too. It will let light flow in from the front entry and help blend the space in the vestibule to the room inside. This way, the vestibule space seems less cramped and guests feel more welcome when they enter your home.

# EXTERIOR VESTIBULE ADD-ON

You'll find this snug vestibule a warm friend on blustery winter days. It fits around your back door, keeping out chilly winds. It will serve, too, as a handsome stash for snowy boots and wet overcoats. And in the summer, this clever addition works equally hard by providing always-needed extra space to store a host of items such as plants and garden supplies.

**1** Before beginning this project, plan your strategies carefully. You can make the unit almost any size, but scale it so that it's in keeping with the rest of the house. Also, unless you have had some experience laying concrete blocks, you should have a masonry contractor lay up the blocks for you.

**2** Measure carefully, then stake out the corners of the foundation. Dig a trench for the footings to a depth below the frost line.

**3** Pour footings in the trench. Allow them to set up, then build the foundation with concrete blocks. Build high enough to have one course of blocks above ground. Fill the cavities in the top course of blocks with concrete and embed foundation bolts.

**4** Lay sill seal atop the blocks, then attach 2x6 sill plates (A—shown; B—not visible) to the foundation. Bolt the sill plates to secure them. Set 2x8s (C,D) atop sill plates as shown; secure.

**5** Nail 2x8 joists (E) to the sill plates and to the skirt. Nail down plywood decking (F).

**6** Construct sidewalls (members not labeled) for the vestibule separately—build them on the ground to make the job easier. Use double studs at corners and around openings for windows or doors. Raise the sidewalls one by one into position on the subfloor and nail them to the 2x8 skirt and to each other. Further attach the walls together by lapping a second top plate.

**7** Build the roof on the ground, too. First build a frame of 2x6s (G,H)—the outer edges of the frame will be flush with finished siding. Then fill in with 2x6 "rafters" (I). Sheathe the rooftop with ½-inch exterior plywood (J).

**8** Nail metal flashing around the perimeter of the roof, then fashion a built-up roof with layers of building paper and tar. Then raise the roof and secure it to the walls' top plates. Make sure roof slopes away from the house.

**9** Run electrical wiring between framing members.

**10** Bolt 2x4 bench supports (K) to the sidewall studs (see sketch). Add brace (L) for more support.

**11** Nail sheathing all around the outside of the walls, leaving openings for doors and windows. Working from the inside, staple insulation between the studs and the roof rafters.

**12** Install the door/window assembly and windows. Caulk around joints for a good seal.

**13** Nail metal or wood siding to the outside walls.

**14** Finish the ceiling and walls with the treatment of your choice.

**15** Nail three evenly spaced 2x4s (M) into place to complete the built-in bench assembly.

**16** Finish the floor with the covering of your choice.

**17** Set the pre-cast concrete steps into position.

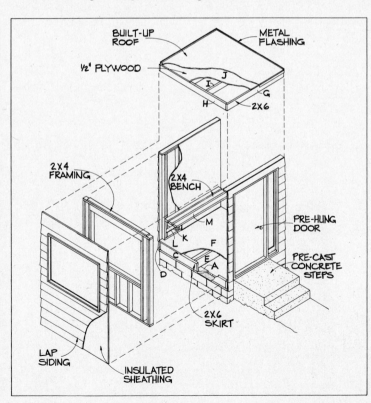

# REMOVABLE VESTIBULE

**Not all energy-saving projects need to be a permanent part of the house. Some—such as this portable exterior entryway—are designed for use only during times of peak drain on your heating or cooling system.**

**1** Plan the dimensions of the structure, keeping in mind that it must fit snugly around the door's trim to form an airtight seal. Also, since many of the unit's components sit on or close to the ground, you should consider investing in pressure-treated wood.

**2** Start by cutting the 2x4s that will make up the sidewalls (A,B,C,D,E). (Note: The studs all are different heights to allow for the slope of the roof. The tops of C and D are angled, too.) Then cut the two stretchers (F) that will tie the walls together.

**3** Lay out all of the 2x4 framing members and face-nail the studs (B,C,D,E) to the sole plates (A).

**4** Connect the two sidewalls at the top by toenailing the 2x4 stretchers (F) to the front and back studs.

**5** Cut 2x4 "rafters" (G) to fit as shown, angling and notching the ends as needed. Then position the end rafters so they are flush with the outside edge of the studs. Nail them to the stretchers and studs. Fill in between the sidewalls with more rafters.

**6** Cover the sides of the enclosure with ⅝-inch exterior plywood siding (H). Cut the siding to match the slope of the roof. Use galvanized nails to attach it to the sidewall studs. Trim the top of the panels with 1x4s (I).

**7** Cut 2x10s (J,K) to face the front of the frame. Nail so outer edge of J,K is flush with 1x4 trim.

**8** Round up a helper and stand up the structure. After positioning it, secure it to the house by driving lag screws through the rear studs. (You may find it helpful to temporarily nail stretchers at the bottom of the unit before moving it.)

**9** Sheathe the roof of the vestibule with a piece of ¾-inch exterior plywood (L). Nail on building paper.

**10** Cover the roof with shingles. Choose shingles that match those already on the roof of your house or, if desired, use a contrasting type such as cedar shingles.

**11** Trim along the front and back edges of the unit with metal flashing. Seal with roofing cement.

**12** Frame the door opening as shown in the detail. Hang a storm door and nail stops (M,N) in place. Install a threshold.

**13** Paint or stain the surfaces of the vestibule as desired. Apply finish inside and outside to help protect the unit both while it's in use and in storage.

**14** Check to make sure that the enclosure is fairly draft free. Tack weather stripping to the frame.

**15** To remove the unit, simply remove the lag screws holding it to the house and move the structure to its storage area.

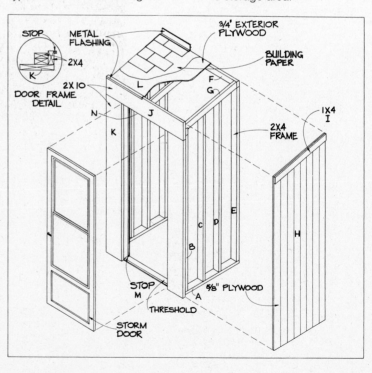

# FOLDING INSULATED SHUTTERS

**Whatever the temperature outside—hot or cold—you can shut out the undesirable with these snug-fitting shutters. A layer of insulation between decorative panels makes this a sensible room addition and a dramatically different window treatment. For a striking effect, cover the shutters with fabric.**

**1** In planning the project, decide whether you want the unit to stand out from its surroundings or blend in with them. Choose your materials accordingly. You may, for example, want to use woods that match your woodwork.

**2** Begin by removing the casing (trim) from around the window you're working with. You'll notice a space between the window's jambs and the wall's surface. If this space doesn't have insulation already tucked tightly into it, fill it with insulation before proceeding to the next step.

**3** If the sill extends beyond the side jambs, cut it off flush with the jambs. If you don't cut it, the projection will interfere with the construction of the new frame.

**4** Construct a boxlike frame with 1x4s (A,B), making sure that it has the same dimensions as the existing jambs. Glue and nail the corners together.

**5** Build another boxlike frame with 2x2s (C,D), making sure that it fits snugly around the 1x4 frame you just built.

**6** Lay the frames on a flat surface, check for a snug fit, and nail them together.

**7** After assembling the frame, lift it into position around the window (you'll need some help with this part of the project), and nail it to the jamb studs.

**8** Nail casing material (E,F) to the 2x2 frame (C,D), making sure it fits snugly against the 1x4 frame (A,B). Use casing nails for this; countersink them.

**9** Cut trim strips (G,H) to face the 2x2 frame (C,D). Using casing nails, nail the strips into place (see sketch detail); countersink the nails.

**10** Butt the corners of the 1x1 shutter stops (I,J) and attach them to the inside of the 1x4 frame (set them back in about 1¼ inches from the front edge).

**11** Build a frame for each shutter panel from 1x1s (K,L) butted together. Use glue and nails.

**12** Fit a piece of ¾-inch-thick rigid foam insulation within each frame. Then, face each side of the shutters with ¼-inch plywood (M). (Note: If you intend to apply fabric to the surface of the shutters, do it before you nail the plywood into place.)

**13** Paint or stain the frame and shutters. Allow to dry.

**14** Assemble the shutters using piano hinges. Then fasten the shutters to the sides of the 1x4 frame as shown.

**15** Fasten door pulls and magnetic latches as shown.

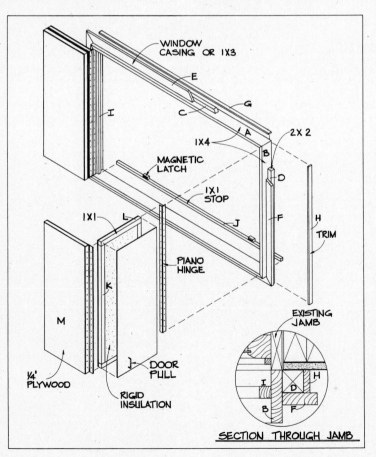

WINDOW CASING OR 1X3

E

G

I

C

A

2 X 2

1X4

B

D

MAGNETIC LATCH

1X1 STOP

J

F

H

TRIM

1X1

L

PIANO HINGE

K

M

¼' PLYWOOD

DOOR PULL

RIGID INSULATION

EXISTING JAMB

I

D

H

B

F

SECTION THROUGH JAMB

# ENERGY-WISE SLIDING DOOR SHUTTERS

**Winter or summer, glass doors are great energy squanderers. If you're the least bit handy, though, you can reduce this waste by installing decorative shutters like the ones that are shown here. They're beautiful—painted, stained, or fabric-covered—and with a hidden layer of rigid foam insulation, they're an effective energy-loss barrier, also.**

**1** When planning this project, keep in mind that the tighter fitting you can make the panels, the better job they'll do for you in terms of saving energy. So accurate measurements are a must.

**2** Start by measuring the width and height of your sliding glass door, including the casing around the doorway. Divide the width by six to get the rough overall size for one shutter panel; then, determine the exact width for each by subtracting the amount of space used by hinges between the panels. For a tighter fit, recess hinges. The shutters should be as tall as the top of the door casing.

**3** Make a frame for each shutter using 1x2s (A,B). First cut rabbets in the 1x2s (see the door panel detail). Then glue and nail the frame pieces together, using butt joints.

**4** Cut a piece of ¼-inch plywood (C) for the back of each panel. Secure with glue and nails. Friction-fit a piece of rigid foam insulation (D) inside the frame. Face the panel with another piece of ¼-inch plywood (C). Secure it with glue and nails. Countersink nailheads and fill with wood putty. (Note: If you plan to cover your shutters with fabric, do it before assembling the panels.)

**5** Paint or stain the shutters as necessary and let them dry.

**6** To construct the surround, first build a header (E,F,G) as shown in the header detail. When cutting pieces for the header, keep in mind that the outside dimension of the surround will be 7 inches wider than the outside dimension of the sliding door's trim.

**7** With a helper, lift the completed header assembly into position above the sliding door casing. Secure the header by screwing 2x2-inch metal angles to the header and to the wall studs (see header detail).

**8** Build the surround's uprights (H,I) as shown in the detail for that part of the construction. Note that the end member (H) is 3½ inches taller than the three other members (I). Position the uprights and secure them by nailing into the header's 2x4s and anchoring at the bottom with metal angles fastened to the floor. Countersink all nailheads and fill with wood putty.

**9** Finish the frame to match or contrast with the shutters.

**10** Hinge each trio of panels together, using three hinges between each panel and its neighbor. Fasten a length of folding door track to the header. Mount heavy-duty folding door hardware following package instructions. Lift the panels into position. To seal air gaps, use foam weather stripping as needed.

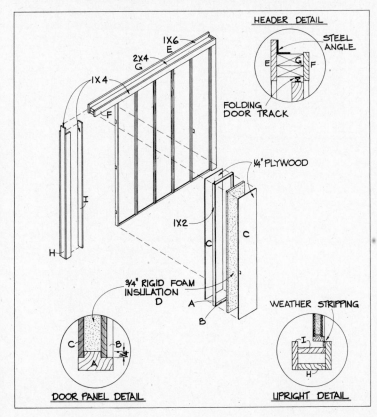

HEADER DETAIL

STEEL ANGLE

1X6
E

2X4
G

1X4

F

FOLDING DOOR TRACK

¼" PLYWOOD

1X2

H

¾" RIGID FOAM INSULATION
D

WEATHER STRIPPING

DOOR PANEL DETAIL

UPRIGHT DETAIL

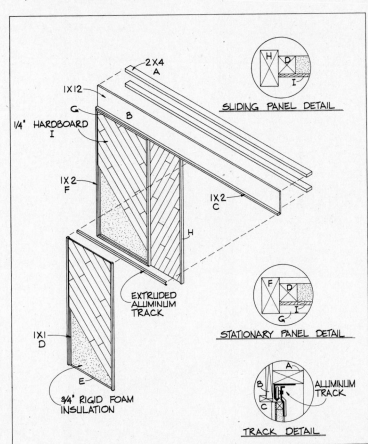

# WHOLE-WALL INSULATING PANELS

During winter, some walls just seem to "radiate" cold air. And cold walls mean more than higher utility bills alone. They also cost you valuable living space because they rob a room of that warm, cozy feeling so necessary in cold weather. So if you have a chill to chase at your place, consider this contemporary solution. Short of adding extra insulation to the sidewalls, there's no better way to handle the problem.

**1** As you can appreciate, the dimensions of this unit can vary considerably, depending on the length and height of the wall you're insulating. So begin by tailoring it to your situation, double-checking all of your measurements and material needs.

**2** Locate the studs in the wall you'll be placing the panels in front of. Then secure two 2x4 nailers (A), using metal angle braces or pre-drilled holes to accommodate lag screws. Place the top 2x4 at ceiling height. Then place the lower 2x4 so that the 1x12 facer board (B) will extend 1½ inches below its bottom edge.

**3** Attach the 1x12 facer board (B) to the 2x4 nailers.

**4** Cut a ¾x¼-inch-deep rabbet along one edge of a 1x2 (C). Attach the 1x2 to the bottom edge of the 1x12 (B) as shown.

**5** Assemble each insulated panel by making a frame of 1x1s (D,E).

Use butt joints, and glue and nail together.

**6** Around the stationary panels, nail a 1x2 frame (F,G)—see detail of stationary panel—mitering the corners for a finished look.

**7** With the sliding panels, attach 1x2s (H) to the panels' sides—see sliding panel detail.

**8** Cut sheets of ¾-inch-thick rigid foam insulation to fit within the frames.

**9** Cover the panels with a facing material of your choice (I), leaving only the 1x2s exposed. The unit shown here sports a handsome covering of ¼-inch hardboard with a simulated diagonal-board surface. However, any type of ¼-inch-thick paneling will work equally well.

**10** Countersink all screws and nails. Stain and varnish all exposed bare wood surfaces on the panels and frame or, if desired, use a good interior enamel paint. If you're painting, fill all nail and screw holes with wood putty before; if staining, fill the holes after doing the staining.

**11** Attach an appropriately sized length of extruded aluminum track to the lower 2x4 nailer (A) as shown in the track mount detail. Be sure that you position the track so the sliding panels will interlock with the stationary panels when closed.

**12** Fasten hanging brackets to the sliding panels, then hang the panels. Slots in the brackets allow for minor adjustments.

**13** Install the stationary panels, screwing or nailing them directly to the 1x2 header (C), the sidewall, and, if desired for more rigidity, the floor.

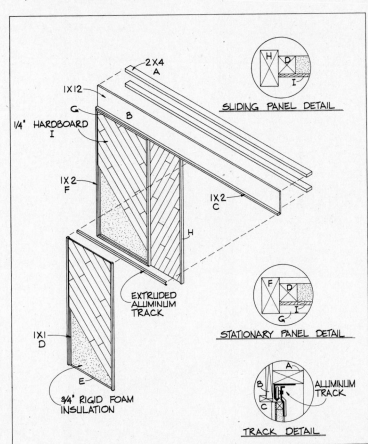

2X4 A
1X12
G
¼" HARDBOARD I
B
1X2 F
1X2 C
H
EXTRUDED ALUMINUM TRACK
1X1 D
E
¾" RIGID FOAM INSULATION

SLIDING PANEL DETAIL

STATIONARY PANEL DETAIL

ALUMINUM TRACK

TRACK DETAIL

# SLIDING DOOR SUPER SHADE

Here's an easy way to solve the often formidable problem of beautifying a sliding glass door. Vertical extensions and a slanted false ceiling surround the glass door like a giant picture frame. And there's an energy-saving bonus, too ... a roll-down shade (the heavy, insulated kind) that hides within easy reach behind the false ceiling. Use the shade to make a dramatic decorative statement in your room.

**1** In planning the dimensions of this project, figure on making the side panels approximately 12 inches wide. This will give the desired look and keep your plywood needs to a minimum. Remember that if you plan to stain the unit, you'll need A-A plywood and 1x2 finish-grade boards.

**2** Cut lengths of ¾-inch plywood (A) to frame each side of the sliding door. Attach them to the frame around the door and, if necessary, anchor each to the wall using metal angles at top and bottom.

**3** Glue and nail a 1x2 facing strip (B) to the exposed raw edge of each vertical. Countersink the nailheads. Stabilize the bottom fronts of the verticals with metal angles positioned behind the 1x2s.

**4** Screw metal mounting brackets above the door trim, then hang the insulated shade. (Buy an insulated shade custom-made to the length you need. Or, design and make your own shade using a colorful fabric lined with a piece of heavy, insulated cloth.)

**5** Attach a 1x2 nailer (C) to the inside surface of each plywood vertical as shown in the sketch. Be sure to allow enough room for the shade to operate smoothly.

**6** Cut another piece of ¾-inch plywood to serve as the false ceiling (D). Miter along the entire length of one edge so it will fit flush against the existing ceiling. Notch back corners as shown. Then angle-cut a 1x2 furring strip (E) as shown in the detail and fasten it to the ceiling to serve as a nailer for the false ceiling.

**7** Slip the false ceiling into position behind the 1x2 facer boards (B). Then nail it to the angle-cut furring strip (E) and to the 1x2 nailers (C). Countersink the nailheads.

**8** To continue the slanted ceiling on either side of the sliding door enclosure as shown in the rendering on page 56, attach furring strips to both the wall and ceiling. Then, cut sections of plywood or drywall and install to match the angle of the false ceiling above the sliding door.

**9** If you plan to paint the enclosure, first fill all nail holes with wood putty, then apply two coats of paint to all surfaces. If you're staining, do this first, then fill nail holes with wood dough, then finish with two coats of sealer.

**10** If desired, dramatize the effect of your completed project by installing track lighting above the entryway. You can use the individual spotlights to highlight your interesting wall hangings, pictures, or hanging plants in and around the enclosure. You might even want to build small shelves for books or curios along the outside of each vertical.

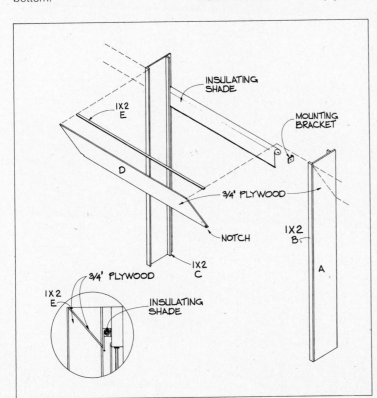

# LEAN-TO SHELTER/ STORAGE UNIT

**Bulky hand and power tools, garden equipment, barbecue suppies ... who couldn't use a little extra storage space for things like these? This roomy stash offers that, and it functions, too, as an attractive shelter for an air conditioner compressor unit.**

**1** When planning the placement of the shed/shelter, check your cooling unit's instruction manual to see what restrictions the manufacturer places on obstructing the air flow into and out of the unit. To function properly, the unit needs an uninterrupted flow of air. Also, work out the dimensions of the unit and the roof pitch that looks most attractive.

**2** Build a base for the storage area by butting together four 2x4s (A,B). Use naturally rot-resistant 2x4s—or lumber that is pressure treated—for the base.

**3** Cover the base with a piece of ¾-inch exterior plywood (C); drill holes through the plywood to allow for drainage.

**4** Next, build a frame for the storage area. Start by nailing 2x4 uprights (F,G,H,I,J) to the sole plates (D,E) You'll have to angle the tops of several of these uprights to allow for the pitch of the roof. Nail the frame to the previously assembled base.

**5** Strengthen the frame by nailing 2x4 crosspieces (K) to the frame.

**6** Notch one end of a long 2x4 (L) to fit against the corner of the storage frame (where F,G,K meet). Use this 2x4 as a pattern to cut an identical board for the other side; then, nail them to the frame as shown. When cutting these members, keep in mind that you don't want the roof to extend so far out beyond the shed that the unit becomes top heavy.

**7** Connect the two boards with two 2x4 stretchers (M). Place one approximately one third of the way up the roof, the other at the ridge of the roof.

**8** Nail on the two roof "rafters" (N), attaching them directly to the uprights of the storage area (I) and to the roof frame (M).

**9** Sheathe the front, sides, and back of the storage unit with ⅝-inch exterior plywood siding (O,P,Q), using galvanized nails. Leave a gap of at least ⅝ inch between the ground and the bottom of the siding to help prevent moisture damage that results from contact between the two.

**10** Cut two pieces of ⅝-inch exterior plywood for the roof (see sketch). Nail the larger piece (R) to the 2x4 framework. Then, attach the smaller roof section (S) with a long piano hinge.

**11** Complete your project by painting it inside and out with a couple coats of good exterior paint. Or, if you wish, stain it with a penetrating stain/sealer. You may want to add a latch and padlock to secure the compartment.

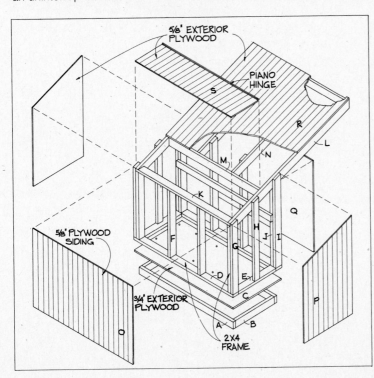

# OPEN-END CENTRAL AIR ENCLOSURE

Though simpler in design and easier to construct than other central air shelters we've shown (see pages 58-59 and 62-63), this open-end version is just as serviceable. In fact, it'll do something the others can't—adapt to the changing seasons. By raising the unit and turning it around, during winter you can take advantage of the sun's warmth (while thwarting the wind), and during summer protect the condensing unit from the harsh rays of the sun.

**1** For maximum use, plan to construct this unit so that all sides are equally wide. If you will be placing it around an already-in-place unit, you'll want to prepare concrete corner pads on which the unit can rest. If, however, the compressor unit is not yet in place, pour a square concrete slab with 3½x 3½-inch notches in each corner to accommodate the 4x4 uprights. Also, check the owner's manual that accompanied the air conditioner or heat pump for any restrictions on blocking air intakes or exhaust.

**2** Cut 4x4 uprights (A) to size and connect them at the top with four 1x6s (B) as shown in the exploded drawing. Miter the corners of the 1x6s.

**3** Separately construct each side panel by nailing 1x8 louvers (C) between two 1x4s (D). Angle the 1x8s to create a louver effect. Fit all three preassembled panels between the 4x4 uprights and secure them to the 4x4s.

**4** Cut another series of 1x8 louvers (E) for the top of the enclosure. Position them carefully, then nail through the 1x6s, into the ends of the 1x8s.

**5** Paint or stain the unit as desired. If you used one of the rot-resistant woods, you can let it weather naturally instead.

**6** If you've set the enclosure on concrete pads, drill a ½-inch hole into the center of each and a corresponding hole in the bottom of each upright. Dowel the two surfaces together with reinforcing rods. For units on notched slabs, drill holes through the 4x4s into the concrete slab. Again dowel with reinforcing rod.

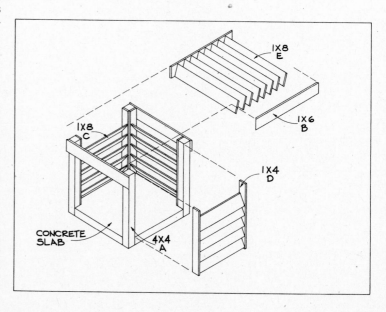

# WINDOW AIR CONDITIONER SHIELD

Window air conditioner units, like their central air counterparts, operate much more efficiently when the sun isn't torturing them with its blistering heat. That's why this project, or an adaptation of it, makes such good sense. Not only is it quite simple to build, but it also is easily removed.

**1** In planning the project, keep in mind that you'll want to size the louvered frame so that it is the exact width of the air conditioner and about 1½ times its height. Doing this will ensure adequate screening without allowing the scale of the project to become too large.

**2** Cut the 1x4 framing members (A,B) to size. Angle the two vertical frame boards (A) at the top and bottom as shown in the sketch. Glue and screw the frame together, using butt joints.

**3** Cut 1x4 boards to serve as louvers (C). Angle each one when nailing to the frame. Space the louvers evenly.

**4** Make armlike supports for the shield (D) from two 1x4s. Cut them long enough so the shield will extend out approximately one foot beyond the air conditioner. Use a coping saw or jigsaw to round the corners of each support on one end (see sketch).

**5** Attach the supports to the shield with sturdy wood screws and glue. Be sure to countersink the screwheads.

**6** Apply the finish of your choice to the unit. If you decide on paint, apply a primer first, then follow with two coats of paint. Or, if you'd rather, treat the wood with penetrating stain or weathering oil to seal out moisture.

**7** Attach the shield supports to the air conditioner housing. Probably the most satisfactory way to do this is to drill pilot holes through the supports and the frame. Then drive sheet metal screws with washers into the pilot holes. This type of screw will grip tight to metal.

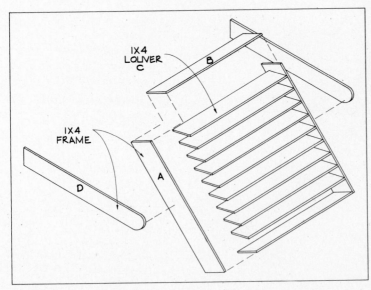

1X4 LOUVER C

1X4 FRAME

B

A

D

# LANDSCAPED CONDITIONER CANOPY

The ideal time to plan a disguise for your central air conditioner or heat pump is *before* you install the unit. That way, you'll have plenty of freedom to harmonize that metal hulk with your overall landscaping design. But even if your unit already is in place, you can adapt this design to suit your needs. This project uses stacked railroad ties and a clever canopy to make the condensor unit less obtrusive. More important, it also shields the unit from the elements.

**1** When planning the location of this project, choose a site that is close to the house, yet removed from day-to-day activities in the yard, if possible. Also, refer to the manufacturer's literature to find out how much space must exist between the unit and any structure next to it. You must take care not to restrict the air flow in or out of the unit.

**2** Excavate a level area and lay a gravel bed for a concrete slab. Plan to pour a slab about four inches thick. If you do the work yourself, be sure to read up on working with concrete before starting. Note: You also can set the unit on concrete blocks.

**3** After pouring and finishing the surface of the slab, let it cure for a week or so.

**4** Stake out locations for the railroad ties.

**5** Excavate as necessary and lay the railroad ties one on top of another to form the corner design you want to achieve. Drive reinforcing rod through the ties' spike holes and into the ground to stabilize the ties. Mound dirt up against the ties to achieve the desired grade. Make sure that you allow for adequate drainage away from the compressor unit.

**6** Miter the corners of three 1x8s (A,B) to form a frame for the canopy. The canopy shown is a right isosceles triangle, so angle the corners of the 1x8s accordingly. Glue and nail the members together.

**7** Cut the 1x8 louvers (C) to size. Start with the shortest one and work your way to the longest, measuring as you go. Rotate each board approximately 10° before nailing in place. Bevel ends of louvers to fit flush with frame. Space the members evenly as you attach them to the frame.

**8** Cut three triangular 1x8 supports (D). Cut three square 4x4 spacers (E). Nail supports to spacers, then nail both to underside of frame A,B. Position the completed frame assembly atop the railroad ties and secure the frame by toenailing to the ties.

**9** If you used redwood, cedar, or pressure-treated wood for this project, you can let it weather naturally, paint it, treat it with weathering oil, or stain and seal it. Paint—or stain and seal—any other type of wood to protect it from the elements.

**10** Complete the project by landscaping around the railroad ties with shrubs, a rock garden, or groundcovers. Climbing vines will soften the rugged look.

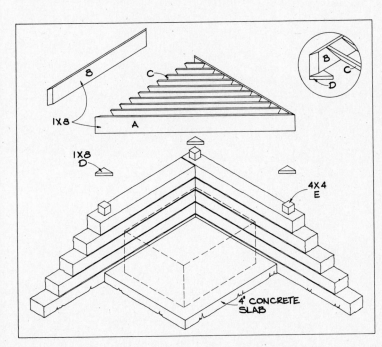

# WRAPAROUND WINDBREAK

**Getting out of the wind is half the battle on cold, wintry days. And this smart-looking project lets you do just that. The structure, which fits around existing door trim, adapts well to many entry situations. And, you'll find it an easy project to build.**

**1** For above-grade entries, plan to extend the windbreak out as far as the edge of the porch. If you're dealing with an on-grade situation, figure an opening at least 42 inches out from the house. The structure should be wide enough to fit snugly around your door's casing. For extra resistance to weather and moisture, you would be wise to choose redwood, cedar, or pressure-treated wood for this project.

**2** Cut one 2x4 upright (A) and three 4x4 uprights (B) to the length needed. Rabbet the tops as shown to accommodate 2x4 top plates. Also rabbet the bottoms of the 4x4 verticals to accept 2x4 soleplates.

**3** Frame around the door by screwing the 2x4 vertical and one of the 4x4s directly to the house. Be sure to use galvanized or other rust-resistant fasteners.

**4** Position a 2x4 top plate (C) above the door casing, fitting it into the previously cut rabbet joints as shown.

**5** Position the remaining two 4x4 uprights (A) and anchor them at the bottom with metal angle supports. (To fasten the supports to the concrete, mark and bore holes in the concrete; fit the holes with expansion anchors and drive lag screws into the anchors.) Connect the uprights by nailing 2x4 soleplates (D,E) between them as shown.

**6** Fit 2x4 top plates (F,G,H) into the rabbet joints on the uprights and nail in place. Note that the 2x4 header (H) over the entryway is turned flat and toenailed into the adjacent 2x4 upright (A).

**7** Cut ½-inch exterior plywood panels (I,J) to form the walls of the windbreak. Nail the panels to the top and soleplates. Add 1x2 stops (K,L) at the top and bottom for more reinforcement.

**8** Use quarter-round strips (M) to serve as stops for the interior vertical surfaces where the panels meet the uprights. Also use quarter-round (N,O,P) to trim around all four sides of each panel on the outside, mitering the corners of the molding as necessary. This trim helps to keep the windbreak walls from rattling in a strong wind and gives the project a finished appearance.

**9** If you used redwood, cedar, or pressure-treated wood for the construction, let it weather naturally, paint it, stain it, or treat it with weathering oil as preferred. For other types of wood, prime, then apply two coats of exterior paint, or lay on two coats of penetrating stain/sealer.

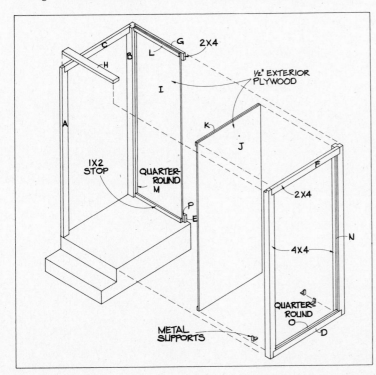

# WINDBREAKING PRIVACY FENCE

All privacy fences have the same mission: to help you create outdoor living areas that are secluded from outside disturbances. This fence does that beautifully. But that's not all. Its angular construction makes it a perfect windshield for the sliding glass door leading into the house, too. Piercing winter winds are redirected and blow harmlessly by.

**1** Carefully plan the location and dimensions of the fence. It should be somewhat wider than the opening you want to shield, approximately six feet high, and as close to the house as is practical.

**2** Cut 4x4 posts (A) to size. Be sure that they're long enough to extend below the frost line to prevent heaving in the springtime. (Frost lines vary from one part of the country to the next. Check with a builder to find out how deep it is in your area.) Unless you are using redwood, cedar, or pressure-treated wood, treat the bottoms and the sides of the posts—wherever the wood will be below ground—by brushing on or soaking in penta (pentachlorophenol). If you brush on penta, pay particular attention to the bottoms of the posts because this usually is where rot begins.

**3** Carefully determine the location of each posthole. Use a posthole digger or auger to dig 8-inch holes to the depth you've already determined is right for your area.

**4** Line the hole's bottom with rocks for drainage, then set the first post and bed it in concrete. (The concrete should extend a few inches above the grade around the post.) Using a carpenter's level, make sure the post is plumb. Set each fence post following the same procedure. As the concrete begins to set around the posts, shape it to shed water.

**5** After the concrete has set up and cured (wait at least one week), connect the posts by toe-nailing 2x4 stretchers (B) near the bottom, halfway up, and at the top. Use galvanized nails to prevent rust stains from streaking the fence.

**6** Separately construct the top portion of the fence by building a frame (C,D,E) as shown in the sketch. Rip the 2x6s to the appropriate width (see detail).

**7** Attach the top portion of the fence to the outside fence posts with angled metal gussets and bolts. Secure the gussets with screws. Building supply center or hardware store personnel can help you locate the metal gussets to do the job.

**8** Complete your fence by cutting wood lath strips to size and nailing them to the frame. You can either butt them together or leave a small space between each. Remember, however, the farther apart you space them, the less windbreaking effect your fence will have.

**9** If you used redwood, cedar, or pressure-treated wood for the fence, you can paint it, stain it, treat it with weathering oil, or let it weather. Other types of lumber must be stained or painted.

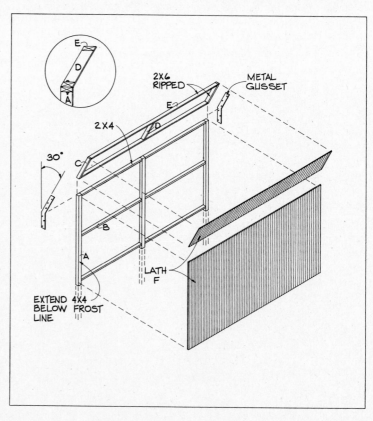

# CONTOURED WINDBREAK

**Crisp lines and stylish details make this windbreak a fine addition to any house. Bend it around a patio or an entryway (as shown here) for privacy and cold weather protection. Then, come summer, flip open the window hatch to let the breezes through. You'll want to landscape around the windbreak with lush groundcovers and evergreens.**

**1** Plan the dimensions of the unit, as well as where you want to place it. For the structure to be most effective, you should build it door high or higher, and place it so it blocks north and west winds, which are always the most troublesome.

**2** Stake out the locations of each 4x4 upright (A).

**3** Find out how deep the frost line is in your area—ask a builder or architect for this information. Then, cut the uprights to the length you need.

**4** Unless you use cedar, redwood, or pressure-treated wood, brush—or soak—the sections of the uprights that will be below ground level in a penta (pentachlorophenol) solution. Set them aside to dry for a minimum of two days.

**5** Using a posthole digger or auger, dig holes of sufficient depth for the uprights. Toss a few rocks down into each hole (the rocks help ensure adequate drainage and keep the post bottoms from making contact with the ground beneath). Position the posts so they are plumb, then set each in concrete. Build up the concrete around each upright to allow for drainage away from the post.

Allow the concrete to cure for a minimum of one week.

**6** Connect the 4x4s with horizontal 2x4 crosspieces (B,C). Miter the ends as necessary to fit the design of your windbreak. Nail in a double 2x4 vertical (D) for the window opening and connect it to the adjacent 4x4 with a 2x4 crosspiece (E).

**7** Cover each side of the structure by nailing up 1x4 or 1x6 shiplap siding (F) at a 45-degree angle. Use galvanized nails. Leave an opening for the window. Trim the siding so it is flush with the windbreak's frame. (Note: You'll want to be sure to stop the siding short of the ground to keep the boards up and away from rot-causing moisture.)

**8** Line the inside of the window opening with 1x6 boards (G,H), mitering the corners as shown.

**9** Using ¾-inch exterior plywood, fashion a cover for the window (I). Then fasten the cover to the frame with hinges (see detail). Fasten a sliding barrel bolt-type lock to the latch side of the cover to hold the cover shut. Rig up a hook-and-eyelet arrangement to hold open the window. (If desired, you can substitute clear acrylic plastic—⅛-inch material will work—for the exterior plywood.)

**10** To protect the wood from the ravages of weather extremes, first fill the edges of the plywood, then apply a penetrating stain/sealer to all of the windbreak's surfaces. Use at least two coats. Or, if desired, you can paint the entire unit with a good exterior house paint. Prime it first with a product that is recommended by the paint manufacturer.

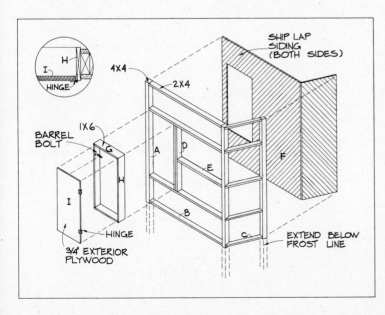

SHIP LAP SIDING (BOTH SIDES)

4X4

2X4

BARREL BOLT

1X6

HINGE

¾" EXTERIOR PLYWOOD

EXTEND BELOW FROST LINE

HINGE

# SUNNY-SIDE WINDOW GREENHOUSE

**Not enough plant display space inside your home? Some of your sun-loving specimens suffering from a lack of natural light? Solve both problems stylishly with this mini-greenhouse add-on. Not only will your greenery appreciate the extra dose of sun they receive inside the hothouse, but you'll benefit, too—the slatted roof helps cut down on heat gain.**

**1** Plan the dimensions of this unit carefully before beginning construction. Allow enough space in the vertical measurements to accommodate the back-to-front slope of the slatted roof. Plan the width of the boxlike base so that your plants will be easy for you to tend.

**2** Build the base first. Start by rabbeting the plant box 1x8s (A,B) to accommodate the plywood bottom to be attached later. Then glue and nail the 1x8s together, using butt joints.

**3** Cut the bottom of the plant box (C) from ¾-inch exterior plywood. Size it to fit flush with the bottom of the 1x8s. Drill ½-inch drain holes in the plywood. Treat it and the inside of the 1x8s with penta to prevent rot. Let dry. Nail the bottom piece to the 1x8s.

**4** Cut two 1x4 verticals for the front of the greenhouse (D) and two longer ones for the back (E). Miter the tops of the verticals to the appropriate angle. Notch the longer verticals (E) to accept the 1x4 roof slat that will butt against and attach to the sidewalls of your house.

**5** Fasten the verticals to the plant box as shown in the sketch. Use glue and screws.

**6** Construct 1x6 "rafters" (F) as shown in the sketch. You'll need to angle-cut each end of the rafters and notch the back end to accommodate the roof slat closest to the house. Then cut the notches for the roof slats. Cut both boards at the same time to ensure matching notches. Fasten the rafters to the uprights with glue and screws.

**7** Cut 1x4 slats (G) to fit into the notches in the rafters. Cut small notches in the bottoms of the slats for drainage. Nail the slats to the rafters.

**8** Build a frame for the front "window" of the unit from mitered 1x2s (H,I) and a 1x4 top piece (J). Notch the ends of the 1x2s as shown so that the 1x4 top piece will fit around the 1x6 rafters. Using glue and nails, fasten the frame members together.

**9** Paint or stain the unit inside and out. Let dry.

**10** Have pieces of ⅛-inch clear acrylic sheet cut to fit the top, sides, and front of the unit. Drill holes in the acrylic and screw the top and side sheets to the inside of the greenhouse as shown. Attach the remaining piece of acrylic to the window frame, then screw the entire frame to the rest of the unit.

**11** Fasten the greenhouse securely to the wall studs of the house, using lag screws driven through the rear 1x8 box member and the rear 1x4 roof slat.

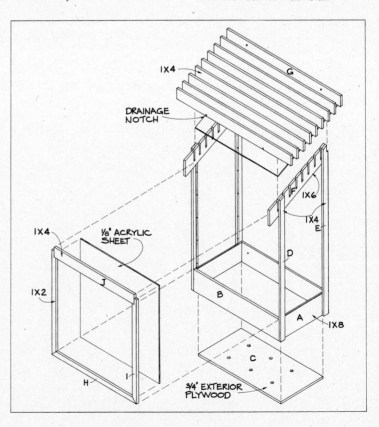

# CUSTOMIZED FIREBOX COVER

**1** Measure the opening of your firebox to determine the dimensions of this project. The 2x4 frame is designed to fit just inside the opening, with foam weather stripping filling any gaps between the frame and the fireplace walls and hearth.

**2** Make a rectangular frame by butting 2x4 verticals (A) and horizontals (B) as shown. Glue and nail together.

**3** Fasten foam weather stripping around the top, sides, and bottom of the frame as shown in the sketch.

**4** Cut a sheet of 1/4-inch clear acrylic (C) large enough to cover the front of the frame.

**5** Using a piece of 2-inch-thick finishing-grade lumber, form the base plate (D). Round the corners as shown, and notch them to fit around the previously constructed framework. Pre-drill holes in the acrylic sheet, and use flat head screws to attach it to the back of the base plate. Countersink screws.

**6** Glue the plastic sheet to the 2x4 frame. Or, if desired, drill holes through the plastic and fasten it with flat head screws.

**7** Miter three pieces of decorative molding (E,F) to serve as trim around the edge of the acrylic sheet. Plan to allow the molding to extend out from the top and sides of the frame far enough to accommodate weather stripping. Glue each piece to the fireplace cover. Tack weather stripping to backside of the molding strips (see detail).

**8** Paint or stain all exposed wood surfaces to blend with the fireplace surroundings and hearth.

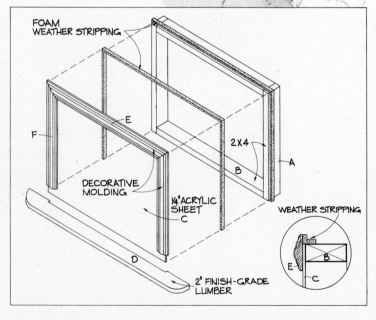

FOAM WEATHER STRIPPING

E

F

2X4

B

A

DECORATIVE MOLDING

1/4"ACRYLIC SHEET

C

D

2' FINISH-GRADE LUMBER

WEATHER STRIPPING

B

E

C

# MAIL SLOT
## COVER

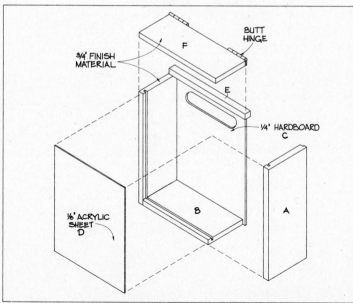

**A small energy leak such as a drafty mail slot is annoying ... and costly! Don't put up with it; instead, solve the problem with this decorative interior mailbox.**

**1** Figure the dimensions of your project. The box shown here is 12x16x6 inches, a good size for most applications.

**2** Cut the sides and bottom of the box (A,B) from ¾-inch finish-grade material. Make a ¼x⅜-inch-deep dado cut in each piece to accommodate the acrylic front panel to be inserted later. Also, rabbet the back edge of the sides to accommodate the hardboard back (see the sketch).

**3** Glue and nail the sides (A) to the bottom (B). Be sure to countersink all nailheads and fill with wood putty.

**4** Cut a back for the box from ¼-inch hardboard (C). Use a keyhole saw or jigsaw to cut an opening to fit the mail slot. Fit the back into the previously cut rabbet joints on the sides of the box. Glue and nail together.

**5** Cut a piece of clear acrylic (D) for the front of the box. Then cut a strip to cap the back top edge of the box (E) and cut the top (F).

**6** Paint or stain the box pieces as desired. Allow to dry.

**7** Insert the plastic front. Glue and nail the cap (E) to the box, countersinking nailheads and filling with wood putty. Touch up with paint or stain as needed.

**8** Using a couple of butt hinges, attach the box top as shown in the sketch.

**9** To hang the unit, drive screws through the hardboard and into the door.

# SLIP-OPEN SKYLIGHT COVER

**Skylights can't be beat for throwing an abundance of natural light into your home. But like all other window openings, they do allow heat to pass through and escape or enter fairly readily. So whenever the** **light filtering through your skylight is not needed, solve the heat loss or gain problem by sliding shut this insulated cover. Later on, you can let the sun in again with just a tug on the draw cord.**

**1** Study the details in the exploded drawing. Keep in mind, too, that you'll want the frame at least twice as long as the cover.

**2** Working on the floor, first miter the corners of four 1x4 boards (A,B) to form a boxlike frame. Glue and nail three sides together, leaving one end open.

**3** Miter the corners of four 1x2s (C,D). Join three of them together and to the 1x4s. Put the remaining piece aside till later.

**4** Miter the 1x1 spacers (E,F). Nail three of them as shown, putting the other piece aside.

**5** Separately put together the fourth side of the frame in a similar fashion, but don't attach it yet.

**6** Cut two more 1x2s (G) for the sides and secure them to the 1x1s (F) and the 1x4s (B).

**7** Fasten 1x1-inch metal angles (H) to the sides of the frame.

**8** To build the cover, fasten the 1x1 framing members (I,J) with glue and nails. Friction-fit a piece of rigid foam insulation (K) in the frame. Face the framing members with hardboard (L).

**9** Rig up the screw eye and cord setup as shown in the detail; insert the cover into its channels and thread the rope.

**10** Fasten the fourth side of the frame. Drill holes in this end to accommodate the rope pulls.

**11** To allow for fastening the unit to the ceiling, drill holes at various intervals up through the 1x4 frame (A,B) and the 1x2s that run perpendicular to them (C,D).

**12** Finish the frame and the cover as desired. Let dry.

**13** Fasten the unit to the ceiling, using long wood screws.

**14** Rig up the pulley system.

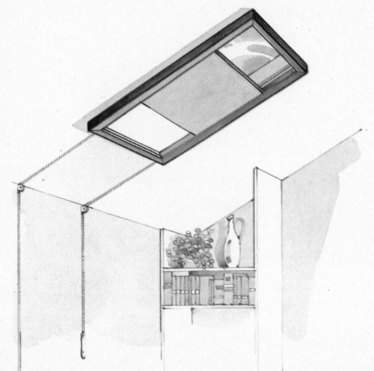

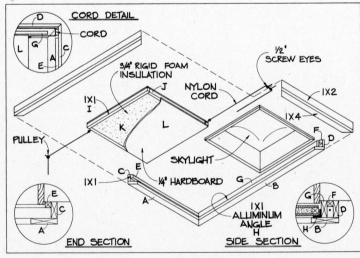

CORD DETAIL

CORD

1/2" SCREW EYES

3/4" RIGID FOAM INSULATION

NYLON CORD

1X2

1X1 I

J

1X4

K

L

F

PULLEY

D

C E

SKYLIGHT

1X1

1/4" HARDBOARD

G

B

A

1X1 ALUMINUM ANGLE H

E

C

A

G F

D

H B

END SECTION

SIDE SECTION

# NO-FRILLS SKYLIGHT COVER

Though there's nothing fancy about this project, it does get the job done. The job is to trap a buffer of air between the skylight surface and the acrylic shield, slowing the passage of heat in or out of your home. Careful caulking and weather-stripping take care of any small energy leaks.

This project has another benefit, too: You can construct the cover and have it in place in just a few short hours.

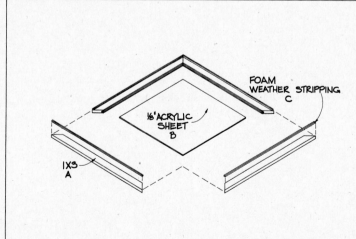

FOAM WEATHER STRIPPING
C

⅛" ACRYLIC SHEET
B

1X3
A

**1** Measure the skylight opening and figure your dimensions accordingly (the skylight shown is square). Ordinarily, the inside of the frame should be flush with the finished opening. The only exception would be if the finished opening trim projects a bit below the ceiling. In this case, you'd want to size the unit so the inside of the frame will butt tightly against the trim.

**2** Cut the 1x3 framework (A), mitering the corners.

**3** Cut a dado ⅛ inch deep on the inside edge of each of the frame's sides. Then, assemble three sides of the frame by gluing and nailing the mitered joints together. (You'll add the fourth side after the acrylic sheet is in place.)

**4** Squeeze a thin bead of caulk into the dado on all sides of the frame. Slide a piece of acrylic sheet (B) into the grooves, wiping away any excess caulk.

**5** Attach the fourth side of the skylight frame by gluing and nailing its mitered corners to the rest of the frame.

**6** Fasten a strip of foam weather stripping (C) to all four sides of the frame as shown to ensure a tight seal.

**7** Raise the skylight cover into position and secure it to the ceiling with screws driven through the frame and into the ceiling. (Skylights always require framing around the shaft, so you needn't worry about not hitting something solid.)

**8** Countersink all nailheads and fill them with wood putty; then stain and seal the frame or, if desired, paint it to match or contrast with the ceiling.

# ENERGY-SAVING PRODUCTS FOR YOU

Ever since the Arab oil embargo of 1973, the conservation of energy has become a major consideration in virtually every facet of American life. This increased awareness of the need to conserve energy led to a myriad of energy-saving products entering the marketplace. Some of these work well; others, not so well.

On the next few pages we present several products that can contribute greatly to your overall energy-saving strategy and in the process lower your utility costs. Keep in mind, though, that unless you first plug up all the holes through which heat escapes and comes into your home, these products won't do the jobs they were designed to do. For more information about how to make your home truly "energy-tight", refer to pages 4-25.

## CLOCK THERMOSTATS

Clock thermostats automatically adjust the temperature settings in your home. During the heating season, they lower the level of heat when it isn't needed, such as when you are sleeping or when no one is home. Lowering the temperature means your heating system has to work less often to maintain the set temperature, and this can save fuel.

The same thing happens in reverse during the cooling season, when the temperature needn't be nearly as cool when you're asleep or absent. (Note: If you own a heat pump, clock thermostats may or may not result in energy savings.)

Of all clock thermostats, you are the least-expensive one. All you have to do is remember to turn down the thermostat when you retire for the night or before you leave home, and turn it back up when you awake or return from work. Two obvious problems present themselves here, though. It's just one more thing you have to do each day. Further, adjusting the thermostat yourself means that the temperature isn't at the level you want it until sometime after you make the adjustment. Most people aren't willing to put up with these inconveniences.

Recognizing this drawback, manufacturers developed automatic clock thermostats. Many of them were designed for installation by do-it-yourselfers and are available through building supply dealers and hardware stores.

You'll find many types of automatic clock thermostats available, each with its own capabilities. The number and types of functions you want your thermostat to perform automatically will directly affect its cost, and in some cases its installation.

Clock thermostats have been on the scene since the 1930s, when they were developed for comfort more than for energy savings. These devices operated off an electric clock, which required that a special wire be run.

### Windup Thermostat Controls

It wasn't until a few years ago, when energy consciousness hit the homeowner in the pocketbook, that an automatic windup thermostat control was developed (A). This device can be wound up like a kitchen cooking timer. You turn the temperature down (or up) by winding up the thermostat. After the specified period of time, it automatically adjusts the temperature. When you leave home or go to bed, you can set back this device for as long as you will be gone or asleep.

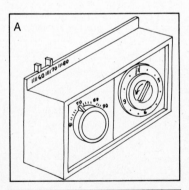
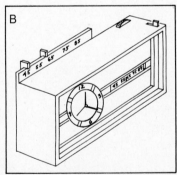
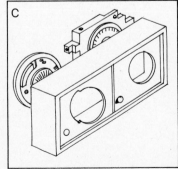
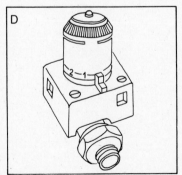

## Battery-Powered Clock Thermostats

Another, even better, way manufacturers circumvented the need to install an additional wire to power an electric clock was to develop battery-powered clock thermostats (B, C). These also can be installed by the homeowner.

## Help for Hot Water and Steam Systems

Thermostatic radiator valves (D), which are available for both hot water and steam systems, attach directly to baseboard convectors or radiators, and control the heat in the room in keeping with the setting on the valve. Although these valves do not operate automatically, they allow a much greater degree of temperature control than the conventional open/closed valves do. Thermostatic radiator valves provide constant temperature in each room and individual zone control, which can mean energy dollars saved.

# GLASS FIREPLACE DOORS

If you're like most folks, the word "fireplace" conjures up images of crackling logs, flickering flames, glowing embers, and good times. Probably the furthest thing from your mind is the amount of energy most fireplaces waste.

But the plain fact is that while the friendly fire you're enjoying roars away, it draws *heated* air from inside your home for combustion and then releases most of it up through the chimney flue. This air must be replaced by additional warm air, which means the heating plant is called on to help.

Perhaps even more costly is the loss of heat that occurs while the fire dies down, when you must leave the damper open. To combat this latter problem glass fireplace doors were developed.

Glass fireplace doors generally come in hinged sections that you can fold to each side to get to the fire. Because they have air ports, which allow air to get to the fire even when the glass doors are closed, the screen can be left shut while a fire is going.

However, when the glass doors are in place they do limit the combustion air getting to the fire, which limits its size. For this reason, and because the doors also limit the radiant heat given off to the living space by the fire, you may want the glass doors out of the way when you are sitting in front of the fire basking in its warmth. Do close the doors and the air ports located at the base of the doors when you leave the room. This not only keeps the heated air where it should be, it also prevents embers from jumping out into the room.

To install glass fireplace doors, follow the instruction sheet that comes with the product.

# STORM-WINDOW KITS

Except for your home's roof, its windows allow more energy to escape than most any other component. And because today the name of the game is controlling the loss of energy, windows deserve your undivided attention.

## Your Options

Your best bet for gaining control of windows is to add a pane of glass. Before, this usually meant you had to install windows on the outside of your house's windows. But today you have an interesting alternative to consider: interior storms (actually clear plastic sheets) that fit snugly against the window trim.

If you don't have conventional storm windows, and you don't want to go to the sizable expense of purchasing them, inside storms make a great deal of sense in terms of money saved. Even if your home already is protected with storms, you may want to add an extra buffer against the elements, especially on windows that face prevailing winds.

## Installation How-To

Unlike combination storm windows, which generally are sold installed, interior storm-window kits are made to cater to the do-it-yourselfer. You'll find these kits available at most large building supply centers. The kit windows are acrylic, and they come in several standard sizes, so be sure you know the size of your window.

To install these windows, first measure the distance from the outside of one side casing to the outside of the other, and from the outside of the top casing to the sill (A). Then subtract enough from these measurements to accommodate the storm's trim strips. These strips fit against the casings. Double-check your measurements; cutting mistakes can't be corrected.

Next, lay the plastic sheet on the floor and mark the proper size on it with a grease pencil. (Leave the protective paper or film in place to protect the surface of the plastic, as it scratches rather easily.) Then, place a wood or metal straightedge along one line and score it by running a knife or other sharp object over it several times (B). Do this for each line.

Place a board, dowel rod, or other object under the plastic and apply light pressure to the plastic. It should separate along the scored line. If not, score the lines several more times and try again.

Next, cut the trim that holds the storm window in place (C). Follow the cutting instructions supplied by the manufacturer of the product you purchased. Your measurements for the trim will be somewhat different from the measurements for the plastic because you must allow for the plastic to sit within the trim. (You can substitute wood molding to hold the panes in place, if you want.)

All that's left to do is to insert the plastic into the trim and to raise the storm into place (D). If your trim strips are adhesive-backed, make sure the casings are clean to ensure a good bond is formed.

Note: When deciding between exterior and interior storms, keep in mind that exterior ones allow you the flexibility of letting in outside air simply by raising the glass. With interior storms, you must lift out the pane.

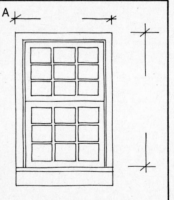

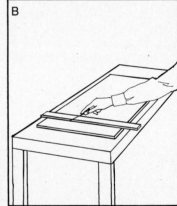

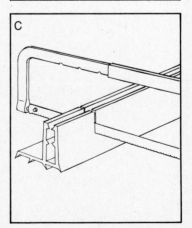

# WATER HEATER INSULATION KITS

Your water heater is probably the least-noticed piece of energy-consuming equipment you have in your home. It just sits there in the utility room, silently doing its job year in and year out. Nonetheless, it could be adding more to your fuel bill than it should.

## How Insulation Kits Save Energy

Raising the temperature of the water that enters your home to a preset level (usually 140 degrees Fahrenheit minimum) accounts for most of the energy expended by your water heater. There isn't much you can do to reduce the energy used here except lower the thermostat setting.

But once the water is hot, the heater must keep it hot. Naturally, the faster the heat escapes, the more often the heater calls on fuel to reverse the process. This is where water heater insulation kits can help you out.

Even though water heater manufacturers stuff insulation in the cavity between the tank and the outer skin, the cool air surrounding the water heater draws heat from within the unit. The colder the surrounding air and the thinner the insulation, the faster that heat flow (loss) takes place.

A water heater insulation kit, acting as another insulative coat, impedes this loss of heat and in the process saves you money.

How much money it saves depends in large measure on where your water heater is. If, for example, it's stationed in an unheated basement or near a cold outside wall, your savings could be considerable.

## Installation Pointers

Installing one of these kits is a do-it-yourself project almost anyone can do. It's basically a cut-and-tape operation.

First measure the diameter and height of your water heater, then mark and cut the insulation (A). If yours is a gas-fired water heater, be sure the insulation doesn't block the pilot light access and the controls. Also, don't allow the insulation to extend down to the floor. You don't want the insulation too close to the burner or close enough to block the air flow that permits proper combustion. For electric water heaters it's perfectly all right to extend the insulation to the floor.

Once you've cut the insulation to fit, wrap it around the heater and secure it with tape as shown (B, C). If you have a gas-fired unit, complete the assembly by running tape strips over the top of the unit (D-1). Don't attempt to insulate the top of the heater. Doing so will block a small space between the top of the unit and the vent pipe known as a draft diverter. This must remain open to ensure safe venting. (Some "low boy" water heaters designed to fit in areas with limited ceiling height, such as a crawl space, have the flue pipe coming out the side. The draft diverter also may be on the side. If you have this type of heater, don't insulate it at all.)

The tops of electric water heaters can be insulated safely. To do this, cut an appropriately sized circle, cut a slit partway through it to accommodate pipes, then position and secure as shown (D-2). Don't insulate the safety valve.

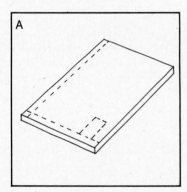

A

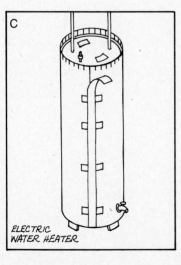

C

ELECTRIC WATER HEATER

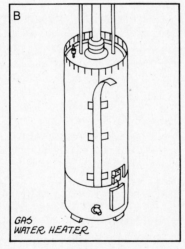

B

GAS WATER HEATER

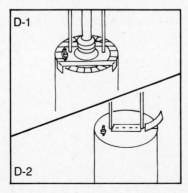

D-1

D-2

# ATTIC VENTILATORS

Well-built houses have a system of vents and louvers that allows air to pass through their unheated upper reaches. This is important year-round, but it' is especially important during the summer months because attic temperatures very often soar to 150 degrees Fahrenheit.

Heat trapped in the upper areas of your house puts additional stress on your cooling system. This makes it harder for your system to keep you and yours comfortable.

## What Ventilators Can Do for You

Although the vent and louver system was built in to help disperse heat (and to help control humidity during the winter), today there are products that help speed the ventilating process. Many companies market power attic ventilators, but all are driven in one of two ways: by wind or electricity.

Wind-propelled turbine ventilators (A) require no electricity to operate. However, they do not turn on and off to meet the specific temperature and humidity conditions in your home.

Electric units, on the other hand, feature an electric fan that is thermostatically controlled to switch on when the temperature reaches a certain point (B, C). Some ventilators come with a humidistat that turns on the fan when the humidity in the attic space gets too high. It's true that ventilators with humidistats cost more than those without them. However, the humidistat makes a power ventilator especially beneficial during cold winter months when moisture can build up in an attic and cause condensation.

## How to Install One

If you already have gable louvers in your home, installing a power ventilator need amount to no more than installing a special fan against one of them. Otherwise, you'll have to mount the unit on your roof (electrically powered units also can be mounted to exterior walls).

When installing either type of power ventilator, you'll want to position it as near the roof's uppermost ridge as possible for maximum efficiency. Manufacturers specify the minimum allowable distance from the ridge. With this distance established, find the center between the rafters and drill a guide hole through this point from inside the attic (D).

Now get on the roof and use the drilled hole as a center point to draw a circle to fit the ventilator you are installing. Some ventilators come with templates to help you draw this circle. Use a saber or keyhole saw to cut out the circle (E).

Being careful not to damage shingles, peel back those around the hole (F). Coat the perimeter of the bottom of the ventilator mounting flange with roofing cement to ensure against leaks (G). Now, position the ventilator over the hole and slip the upper half of the flange under the raised shingles (H). The lower half goes on top of the shingles.

Nail the fan's flange to the roof decking with roofing nails, and caulk all the way around (I). Seal all edges with roofing cement.

To complete the installation, connect the fan's wires to your home's circuitry. If you haven't had much experience running wiring, call in a contractor. The cost shouldn't be prohibitive.

Note: For more information on the importance of having adequate ventilation in your home, refer to pages 10 and 11.

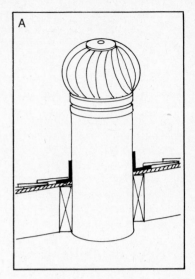
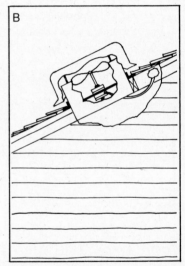
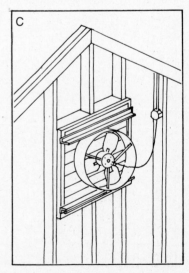

81

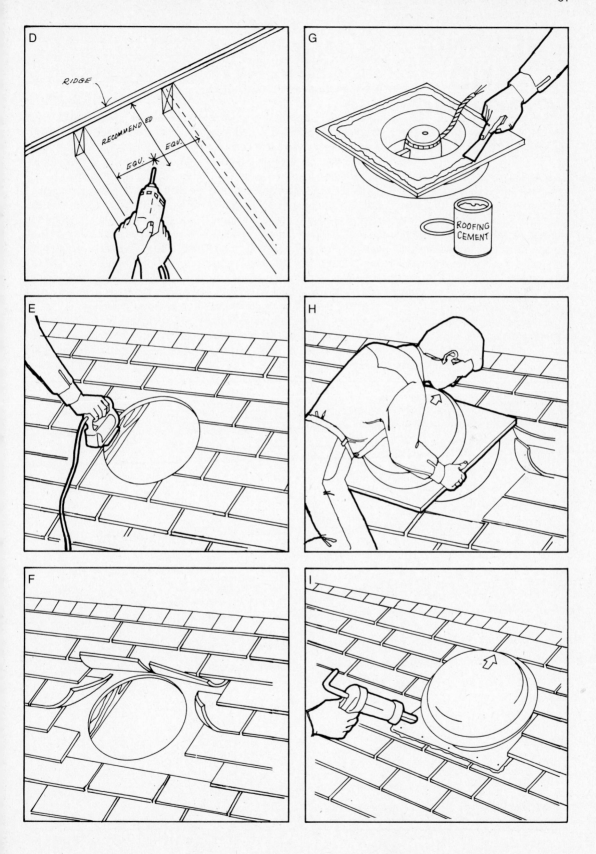

# HEATING AND COOLING EQUIPMENT

The heating and cooling equipment that keeps your home comfortable regardless of the temperature outside constitutes the hardest working system in your house. Yet, if you are like most of us, you almost forget it's there. The reason: Most systems give trouble-free service year after year, and seldom act up.

But your space conditioning equipment (as the furnace and air conditioner sometimes are known) deserves a little attention

from time to time. Although the equipment may continue to run even if you neglect it, it won't operate as efficiently as it would if you took proper care of it. And, efficient operation means money saved when the fuel bill arrives. Maintaining your space conditioning equipment also can extend its life, and this can save you a bundle over the years.

Reading this last section of the book will help you in several ways. First, you'll learn a little bit about heat and how various systems move it through houses. Second, you'll learn how to keep your equipment in tip-top shape as well as how to improve your system. And finally, after reading this material, you'll be in a better position to make a wise decision when it comes time to replace your present power plant.

## HOW HEAT BEHAVES

There's a lot of talk about heat these days—how to keep it out of a home, how to keep it in, and how to save money and energy generating it. This is why it's important to understand heat.

Actually, heat is a form of energy that can neither be created nor destroyed, merely changed in form. And this is where your heating and cooling equipment comes into the picture. It takes advantage of heat's tendency to seek cooler areas to heat or cool the air in your house.

For example, when you turn up your thermostat to increase your heat, the furnace or boiler heats the air or water and sends it out to

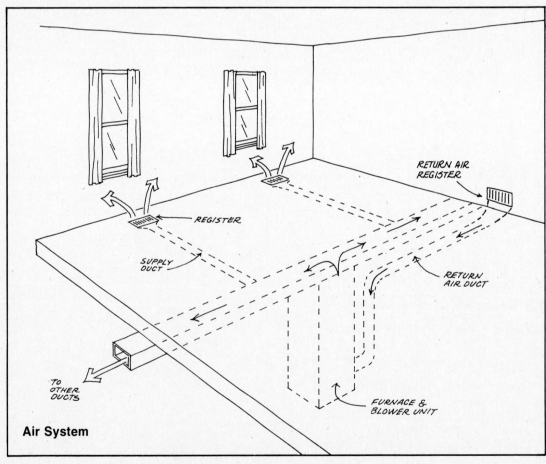

**Air System**

circulate throughout your home. As it circulates, the hot water or hot air releases its heat to the cooler air in your home. The air or water, now cooler, then returns to the heat source (furnace or boiler) to be warmed once again. Air conditioning follows this same principle, only in reverse.

# COMMON HEATING SYSTEMS

There are two common types of heat distribution systems (see the anatomy drawings on this and the facing page). Air or "ducted" systems distribute warm or cool air by means of a network of ducts that run vein-like throughout your house. "Piped" systems, on the other hand, use pipes to carry the hot water or steam.

## Air Systems

All air systems have two sets of ducts. One set, the "supply" ducts, carry the treated air from the furnace to the distribution registers throughout the house. The second set of ducts, the "return" air ducts, return the room air to the furnace for further treatment.

Older homes frequently have "gravity" systems to distribute heat and to return air to the furnace. They operate on the old "warm air rises, cool air falls" principle. Newer homes have forced-air systems, which have a furnace that includes a blower to boost the flow of air throughout your home.

## Piped Systems

In piped systems, water (either in the form of liquid or steam) serves as the heat distribution medium. Piped systems can be gravity or forced also. Gravity piped systems take advantage of the fact that water expands as it heats up.

Forced hot water systems, also known as hydronic systems, use a pump to circulate the hot water. The pump serves the same basic purpose that the blower serves in a forced-air system.

Steam systems usually employ a "one-pipe" distribution system, which means that a single line serves as both supply and return for each radiation unit. Most all hot water systems use a "two-pipe" arrangement, whereby water enters and leaves the radiation units via separate pipes.

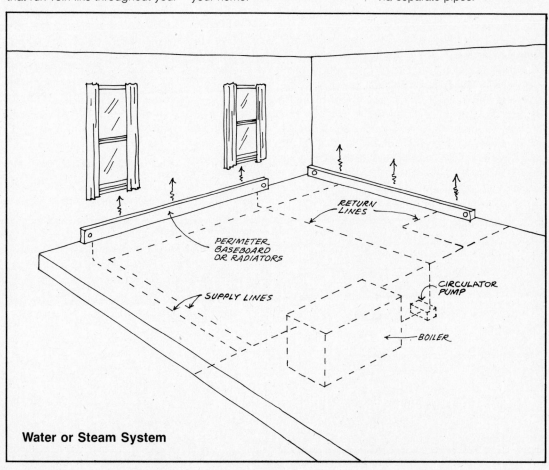

RETURN LINES

PERIMETER BASEBOARD OR RADIATORS

SUPPLY LINES

CIRCULATOR PUMP

BOILER

**Water or Steam System**

# KNOWING HOW A FURNACE OPERATES

Homes that have a ducted distribution system depend on a furnace—gas-fired, oil-fired, or electric—to "make" heat. In order for you to have a better understanding of how your particular power plant works, the following few pages take a close look at the various types of furnaces that are available.

## How Furnaces Work in General

All furnaces have the same basic design, although their burners or heat sources may vary. Generally, a furnace is a box within a box. The outer box forms a protective shell for the inner box, which exchanges the heat.

In the case of gas or oil furnaces, the burners are inside the heat exchanger, which is vented to the outside via a flue pipe and chimney. Unless the furnace needs repair or replacement, the air coming through the return air duct from inside your home to the furnace for conditioning never comes into contact with the combustion air inside the heat exchanger.

When your thermostat calls for heat, the burner kicks on and begins heating the heat exchanger. Once the heat exchanger is warmed to a factory-set temperature (for example, 110 degrees Fahrenheit), a thermocouple tells the blower to come on. The blower pulls air in through the return air ducts, then blows it across the outside surface of the heat exchanger, warming the air. The warmed air then is transferred throughout your home via the supply ducts.

Once the house reaches within a degree or two of the temperature you have set on your thermostat, the burner shuts down, but the blower keeps going. The reason: The heat exchanger still has a lot of heat in it. To take advantage of this heat, there is a separate blower-off thermocouple, that shuts down the blower only after the heat exchanger reaches a preset temperature (usually about 95 degrees Fahrenheit).

Besides the blower-on and -off thermocouples, furnaces also have a built-in safety feature known as a limit switch, which is set at the factory. If for any reason the heat exchanger temperature rises to a point beyond the temperature determined by the manufacturer to be a safe limit, the burner automatically shuts down, even if your thermostat is still calling for heat. Under no circumstances should you ever tamper with this switch.

Gas and oil furnaces, because they burn fossil fuels, which give off noxious fumes, require venting to the outside. A flue pipe, which connects the furnace to the chimney, allows the needed ventilation. The flue should slant at an upward angle as it runs from the furnace to the chimney (A). This way, the hot gases can flow easily inside the pipe to the chimney. If the pipe is level or slanted in the wrong direction, the gases could vent into your house instead of up the chimney.

As you can see from the sketch, the normal flow of harmful gases can be impeded in a number of ways. So it is vitally important that you check each season for obstructions and clean (sweep) the chimney occasionally. Cleaning is important especially if you have an oil furnace, which causes more deposits than does a gas furnace.

## Gas Furnaces

Gas furnaces and oil furnaces differ surprisingly little (see the

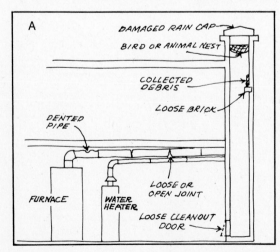

A
DAMAGED RAIN CAP
BIRD OR ANIMAL NEST
COLLECTED DEBRIS
LOOSE BRICK
DENTED PIPE
LOOSE OR OPEN JOINT
FURNACE
WATER HEATER
LOOSE CLEANOUT DOOR

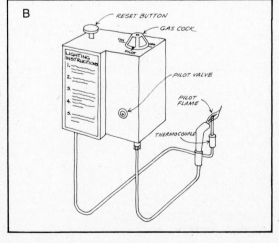

B
RESET BUTTON
GAS COCK
LIGHTING INSTRUCTIONS
1.
2.
3.
4.
5.
ON
PILOT
PILOT VALVE
PILOT FLAME
THERMOCOUPLE

anatomy drawings), but their burners do behave somewhat differently. The burners on a gas furnace resemble those atop a gas range—they're just bigger and more numerous.

Most gas furnaces have pilot lights (B), although some of the newer ones have automatic spark ignitors similar to those that are found on other recent-model gas appliances such as ovens and clothes dryers.

One of the most common problems with gas-fired furnaces is that the pilot light sometimes goes out. So, if your furnace fails to function, check the pilot light before calling a serviceman.

Procedures for re-lighting a pilot differ somewhat, so follow the steps listed on the instruction plate attached to the furnace or pilot light assembly. With most furnaces, you'll find a gas cock with three settings on it—OFF, PILOT, and ON.

You turn the cock to OFF, wait a few minutes for any residual gas to clear, then switch to the PILOT setting. Hold a match to the pilot, depress a reset button, and hold it down for the amount of time that is specified on the furnace's instruction plate.

If the pilot stays lit, turn the cock to ON. If the pilot goes out again after you release the reset, repeat the entire procedure. If this doesn't work, it's time to call a serviceman.

It is a good idea to call a serviceman every other year just before the heating season to have him check things over. He also should clean the gas burners for you because rust and scale eventually clog some of the burner orifices, reducing their efficiency. Cleaning the burners isn't a big job, but you do run the risk of jarring the shutter settings on their manifolds, and adjusting these calls for an expert's eye to get the flame right.

## Gas Furnace

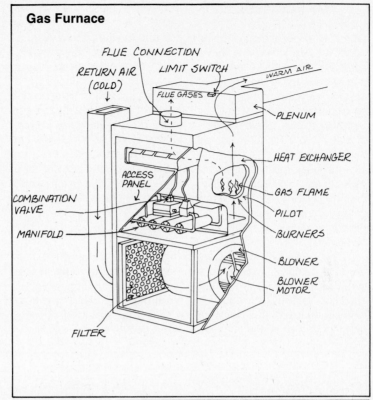

## Oil Furnace

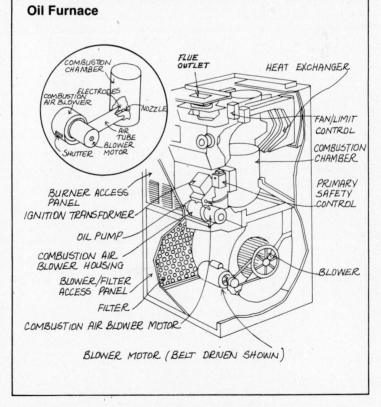

## Oil Furnaces

Oil furnaces (see the anatomy on page 85) are somewhat more complex than gas furnaces, mainly because of the nature of the oil burner itself. In most cases, an oil furnace burner contains a blower of its own. When the thermostat in your home demands heat, the burner mixes oil and air—much as the carburetor of your car mixes air and gasoline. An electric spark then ignites this combination, and the blower on the burner shoots the flame into a combustion chamber.

Although modern oil burners are very complex, they provide surefire heat. However, the burners do require a regular—normally monthly—maintenance program and an annual tune-up.

Neglecting these can greatly undercut the burner's efficiency and add to your oil bills. Neglect also could lead to costly repairs.

Servicing requirements vary, so check the manufacturer's literature for specifics. Nonetheless, some of the things that need to be done periodically include changing the oil filter, cleaning the fan blades, and lubricating the burner motor. Also, call for a tune-up by a professional just before each heating season.

## Electric Furnaces

Though similar in design and operation to both gas- and oil-fired furnaces, electric furnaces (A) differ in that they don't have burners, but a series of electric-resistance heating elements.

The number of heating elements in an electric furnace does vary, but generally there are between two and five. During operation, these elements phase in one at a time until they satisfy the demand for heat.

As already mentioned, electric furnaces don't require venting because no combustion occurs. One advantage in this is that you can place the unit almost anywhere; you're not limited to placing it near a chimney.

Besides being a convenient heat source for a central heating system furnace, electric heat also is adaptable to two other heating configurations that are sometimes used in the home. One is radiant heating.

It consists of electric-resistance cables embedded directly

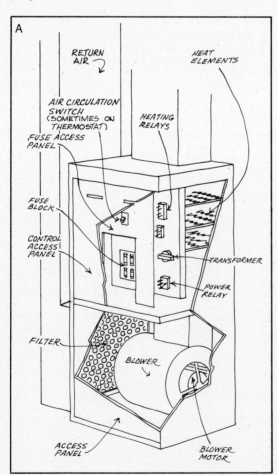

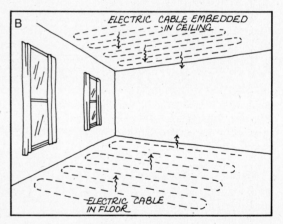

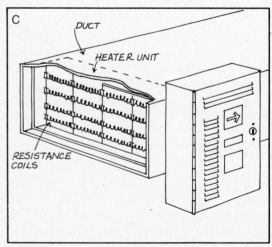

in the floor or ceiling of a room (B). This is not the least-expensive way to heat a home because of the cost of electricity as compared with other fuels in your area. Nonetheless, it is efficient because radiant systems have individual controls for each room. If a room is not in use, you can turn off the heat without affecting other rooms in your home. This cannot be done as conveniently with systems that rely on a central furnace or boiler.

The second adaptation involves the use of electric-resistance duct heaters in conjunction with the forced-air system to provide individual zone control (C). They are merely electric-resistance coils that are made to be installed in the supply-air ducts of forced-air systems.

# KNOWING HOW BOILERS WORK

Hot water and steam boilers do have their differences but, as with furnaces, not as many as you might imagine. For example, both hot water and steam heating systems employ the same types of boilers. Also, either system can be fired by gas or oil burners, or electric-resistance elements.

A steam boiler (D) functions in much the same way as a giant tea kettle, except that in a boiler the water doesn't just sit there idly waiting to be heated. Instead, it circulates around the heat source through a jacket or tubes.

Generally, boilers have gauges and control valves that let you keep an eye on the pressure within the system and that allow the boiler to be controlled either automatically or manually. Steam systems have a low-water cutoff control that shuts down the system if the boiler's water level gets dangerously low. Some even have an automatic feed that supplies fresh make-up water.

Hot water boilers (E) have an expansion tank that must be properly charged with air to prevent the water from boiling.

If you have a forced (hydronic) water system, it will include one or more pumps situated on the return lines near the boiler. Some of these motors need periodic lubrication; others do not. Be sure to check to see which category your motor falls into, and oil if necessary.

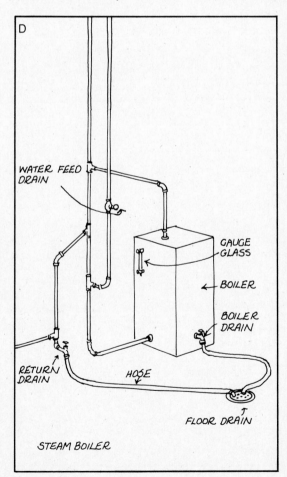

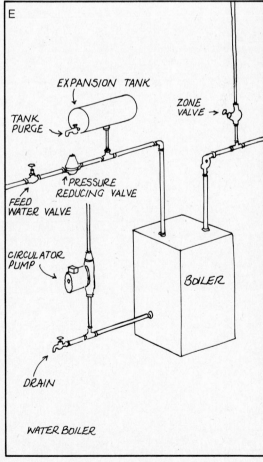

# THE VERSATILE, ENERGY-WISE HEAT PUMP

If you've ever stood outside near your air conditioner compressor as it worked away, you've undoubtedly noticed that the air coming from it is hot. That's because an air conditioner has the ability to collect heat from inside your home, carry it outside, and release it. A heat pump has the same ability, plus another, extraordinary one. By means of a re-versing valve, a heat pump also can collect heat from cold, win-tery air and move the heat inside. (As surprising as this may seem, air at 0 degrees Fahrenheit con-tains 80 percent of the heat avail-able in air at 100 degrees Fahrenheit.) This unique feature makes a heat pump the only single piece of equipment that can both heat and cool a home.

## How It Works

How does this mechanical marvel work? Basically, it operates on the flow of a refrigerant that passes through a series of coils. At differ-ent temperatures and pressures, the refrigerant changes states from a liquid to a gas and back again. As it does so, it either gives off or takes up heat. (See the dia-grams below depicting the flow of refrigerant in both the heating and cooling modes.)

There is something of a prob-lem with the heat pump system, however. As the outside tempera-ture decreases and the need for heat inside increases, the effi-ciency of the heat pump de-creases. When the outside tem-perature gets to a point that the pump can't handle the load by ex-tracting heat from outdoors, con-

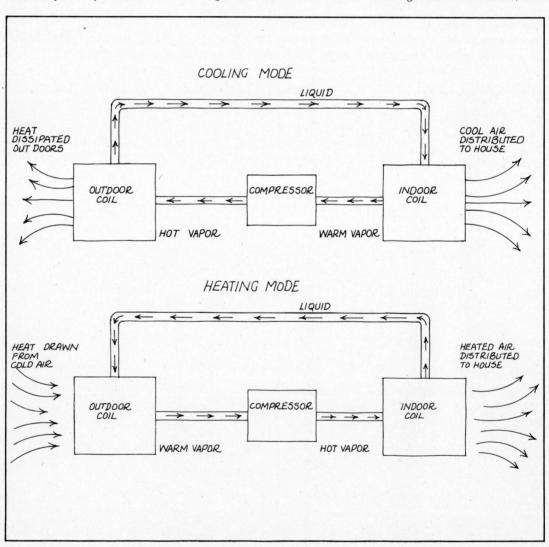

ventional electric-resistance heating coils kick in one at a time to take up the slack. These coils increase the heat level of the air being circulated through the home. Heat pump-generated air is significantly cooler.

## Heat Pump History

The idea of heat pumps, innovative as it sounds, really isn't new. Heat pumps have been around since the 1930s. But because of equipment problems, and partly because the timing just wasn't right, they never really caught on. With the energy crisis in the early 1970s, though, and the natural gas moratoriums in many parts of the country, heat pumps sparked renewed interest. New homes could not receive natural gas hookups, and often the only alternative builders had was to use electricity.

The concept of heat pumps now seems to be an idea whose time has come. Manufacturers are offering warranties on their equipment, indicating they think it will hold up. When you select a heat pump, carefully study the warranties offered and make sure the manufacturer is standing squarely behind his product.

## How to Choose One

If you're in the market for a heat pump, you should realize that not all heat pumps are equally efficient. Each model has two rating numbers, the importance of which should not be overlooked. One number designates the heating efficiency (the coefficient of performance—COP); the other, the cooling efficiency (the energy efficiency ratio—EER). Both numbers indicate the amount of energy put out by the pump divided by the amount put into it.

For example, if a particular heat pump pulls 12,000 BTUs of electricity and puts out 36,000 BTUs of heat, then the COP of that machine is three. In practical dollars and cents terms, what this means is that if you are using this particular heat pump to heat your home, you would have to pay one-third what you would have to pay if the same house were heated by standard electric-resistance heating methods. The higher these rating numbers, the more efficient the unit. Keep in mind, however, that the COP and EER ratings are maximums at ideal temperatures.

Most residential heat pumps are of the split-system type (see the anatomy drawings). The outdoor unit resembles the conventional air conditioning compressor unit that sits outside your home. Inside, an air handler—which contains the cooling and heating coils, a blower, and a series of electric-resistance heating coils—distributes conditioned air via a network of ducts.

The single-unit system has all the components housed in the unit outside. Only the supply and return-air ducts penetrate the exterior walls.

If your house currently has an air distribution system with a conventional furnace, you may want to consider a heat pump when you have to replace your furnace.

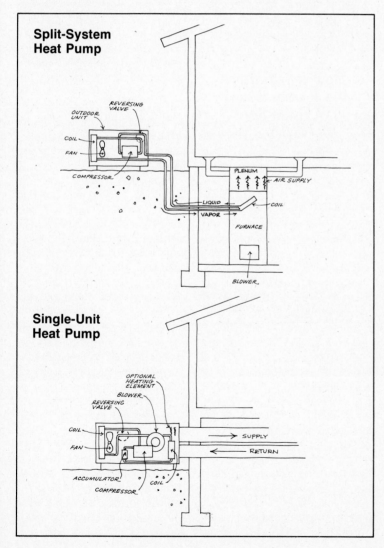

**Split-System Heat Pump**

**Single-Unit Heat Pump**

# HUMIDITY AND COMFORT

Humidity (or the lack of it) does strange things to the air in your home. During the hot summer months, if the humidity level is too high, the air will *feel* warmer than it actually is. In the wintertime, humidity levels drop off considerably, making the air *seem* cooler.

Your reaction to either of these situations is predictable: You adjust your thermostat setting to compensate for too much or too little humidity. Not surprisingly, you pay for your indulgence when you pay your utility bills.

## Why Humidity Affects Us the Way It Does

When your body perspires, it does so to help get rid of excess heat, thereby keeping you cool. Water forms on your skin, and the air passing over the skin evaporates the liquid. The higher the humidity (or amount of moisture present in the air) the harder it is for your perspiration to evaporate. And the slower it evaporates, the hotter you feel. That's why it's important to have the proper level of humidity present year-round.

## Signs of a Humidity Imbalance in Your House

The surest way to determine whether you need to change the humidity level is to buy a hygrometer, a device that measures relative humidity. But generally you can "feel" the need without going to this expense. In the summer, a musty smell in basements or other areas signals too much humidity. In the winter, excessive static electricity and dry

| WINTERTIME HUMIDITY SETTINGS | |
|---|---|
| OUTSIDE TEMPERATURE | INSIDE HUMIDITY |
| −20F | 15 to 20% |
| −10F | 20 to 25% |
| 0F | 25 to 30% |
| +10F | 30 to 35% |
| +20F | 35 to 40% |

throats will tip you off to too little humidity. Note: Although you won't be able to see it at first, a humidity deficiency also is very hard on furniture.

## How to Maintain the Proper Level of Humidity

How you do this depends largely on the season of the year. During the summertime, you want to keep the humidity level down. That is one of the things an air conditioner does best. (If you have an air conditioner—either a window or central unit—you've undoubtedly noticed water as it was dispelled from the unit. That water is condensation formed when the water in the air is removed to decrease the humidity.) If you don't have air conditioning, or if your air conditioner by itself can't handle all the humidity that is present in your home's air, get a dehumidifier.

Conditions reverse during winter when the humidity isn't nearly as high. If your home is tightly constructed, it is possible that the moisture created by everyday activities will be sufficient to keep the humidity level in your home at a comfortable level. In fact, you may even find it necessary to get rid of some of the humidity. You

can do this by ventilating as much as possible. For example, be sure to turn on bathroom ventilating fans when showering, make sure the clothes dryer is properly vented outdoors, and install a vent hood over the range if you don't already have one.

In most cases, however, you will find that to maintain a proper humidity level during the coldest days of winter, you'll need to add humidity to the air.

If you don't have a forced-air distribution system, you can add humidity easily with a free-standing humidifier available in any appliance store. Providing your home isn't too exceptionally spacious, such a humidifier centrally located should be enough to provide humidity throughout your home.

If you do have a forced-air system in your home, it's wise to install a humidifier in the supply air duct (see the opposite page for installation pointers).

Regardless of the type of humidifier you decide on, they all come with a dial of some sort that lets you control the level of humidity in the air. Be sure you use it to set the proper humidity level as indicated in the chart above. The settings are calculated for a home with insulating glass or storm windows.

## Choosing and Installing a Power Humidifier

Although all power humidifiers have the same mission, not all of them accomplish it in the same way. Some spray a fine mist directly into the air stream; others rotate a porous water wheel through the heated air; still others pull the air through a moist pad.

Better units are controlled by a *humidistat*—a moisture-sensing device similar to a thermostat. When the air's relative humidity reaches a preset point, the humidistat turns off the humidifier until the moisture level drops again. The unit also cycles on and off with the furnace blower.

Installing a humidifier involves cutting a hole in a plenum or duct, hooking into a cold water line, and piping any overflow to a nearby drain. You also must make electrical connections to 120-volt house current, the furnace's low-voltage transformer, or both.

Most power humidifiers mount on the furnace plenum, as illustrated here. A few, however, attach to the main return, or to a bypass between the two. Consult the manufacturer's instructions before installing these.

Most units come with a template you tape in place to position the unit (A). Choose a spot you can get to easily for service. After positioning the unit, cut an opening in the duct with a pair of aviation snips (B). You also will have to drill holes for the mounting hardware. Next, slip the mounting collar into place and secure it with sheet metal screws (C). Caulk its flange for an airtight fit.

As you assemble the humidifier, make sure that the arrow on its solenoid valve points in the same direction as the water flow (D). When you connect the water line, provide a shut-off valve so you can easily remove the unit if it ever needs servicing (E). Situate the humidistat on the main return duct (F). Check the manufacturer's instructions for information about how to wire the unit.

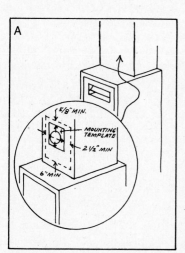

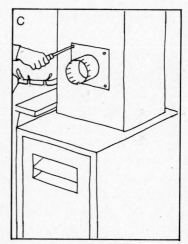

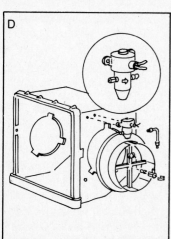

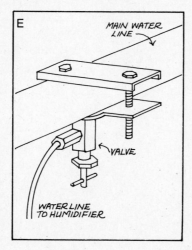

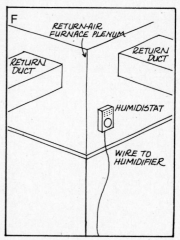

# THERMOSTATS

Your heating/cooling system's thermostat, the command post from which all orders for conditioned air originate, rarely requires attention. In fact, it may never give you any difficulty. But in the event that it is thrown off or malfunctions occur, the result affects not only your comfort but also your fuel bill.

So it just makes good sense to know a little bit about this important device, as well as the things that can affect its operation. As you're about to see, some problems are easily remedied by you; however, others are best left to a furnace serviceman.

## How They Work

Basically, a thermostat is an on/off switch for your furnace that reacts to your request for a change in temperature. Inside is a coil or strip of two metals, each of which expands and contracts at different rates at the same temperature. In some thermostats, these metals make contact with each other and cause a capsule containing mercury to tip, opening or closing the circuit (A).

In other thermostats, contact points, much like those found in the distributor of your automobile, accomplish the same function as the metal coils do (B).

## Troubleshooting Your Thermostat

If you suspect that your thermostat isn't working quite right, first make sure you haven't positioned any furniture or heat sources, such as lamps and televisions, where they could throw off this rather sensitive device. The thermostat should be free to detect the average temperature in the room.

If no furniture or heat source is affecting your thermostat, remove any dust that may be inside the thermostat. To clean the insides, remove the cover. For a coil-type unit, clean by stroking the coil lightly with an artist's brush. If yours is a contact-type unit, clean the contacts by running a plain white piece of paper between the closed contacts (B). Clean the rest of the inside of either type thermostat with an artist's brush or a brush with an air bulb on the end of it, just like those that are used to clean delicate photographic lenses.

It is also a good idea to make sure the thermostat is level. This is important to the proper operation of the unit, especially if it is of the mercury-bulb type.

To do this, look around for a "level" line on the body of the thermostat, or for a set of pins that were obviously put there to hold a level. With some thermostats you may have to remove the working assembly held in place by some screws to get to the leveling pins.

Once you have found the level line, check with a level and make any adjustment by loosening the mounting screws and turning.

You also should test the accuracy of your thermostat by taping a thermometer on the wall near the thermostat (C). If there is a discrepancy between the two, call in a serviceman.

Don't attempt to re-calibrate the thermostat yourself. There is a series of adjustments that need to be made to both the furnace and the thermostat, which work in concert. Such adjustments should be made by someone thoroughly familiar with the system and the ramifications one adjustment will have on other parts. If you make these adjustments yourself, you risk throwing off the whole system.

Another device that can foul up the operation of the thermostat is the anticipator (D). This thermostat part controls the length of the burner cycle on your furnace. If there is little fluctuation in temperature in your home between furnace cycles, there is no reason to change the adjustment of the anticipator. But, if you feel a significant change in temperature, you may want to call a serviceman to check the anticipator.

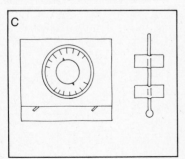

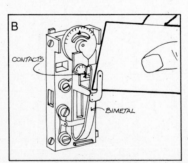

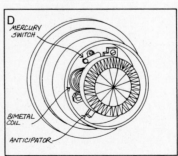

# FURNACE MAINTENANCE

Although most maintenance and adjustments on your heating system should be done by a professional, there are several things you can and should do to keep your system in tip-top form.

## Change the Filter

Air distribution systems use air filters to remove dust particles from the air as it approaches the blower through the return ducts.

The more dirt the filter contains, the harder your furnace must work to get air through, and that costs you energy. Also, in extreme cases, a clogged filter can cause the furnace to overheat, in which case the safety limit switch will shut down the unit.

To keep your furnace operating efficiently, you should change or clean your furnace filter once a month during use. (Some furnaces have permanent filters that you remove and clean.)

To change the filter, first turn your thermostat to OFF; then turn off the master power switch to the furnace. Next, slide out the old filter (A).

Most disposable filters are oil-treated fiber glass in a cardboard frame. Before inserting a new one, be sure to locate the arrow showing which way you should place the filter in the furnace in relation to the air flow. The air should strike the oiled side first.

Other furnaces have a so-called "hammock-type" filter positioned to the sides of and beneath the blower. This kind of filter is easy to remove and replace.

## Servicing the Blower

Make blower maintenance a seasonal habit with you. Before each period of use, lubricate the blower (B) and the blower motor.

Generally, both the blower and the motor require lubrication, and sometimes the type of oil required for each is different. For example, some manufacturers specify SAE 10 weight oil for the motor and SAE 30 for the blower itself. Sometimes, these requirements are spelled out on a label attached inside the blower housing. Or look in the service manual. If you cannot find the information, call your heating contractor and ask him. Then oil accordingly.

Be sure not to over-lubricate because the centrifugal force of the blower and motor could splash oil throughout the housing, causing quite a mess. A few drops is usually enough. Again, check the specifications for your equipment. You'll find the oiling ports at each end of the blower and at motor shafts where the bearings are.

Some blowers have grease cups that provide lubrication (C). With this type, refill them with bearing lubricant once a year.

## Adjust the Belt

Some blowers have direct-drive motors; others use a V-shaped fan belt that goes around pulleys on the blower motor and the blower itself (D). The direct-drive type shouldn't need adjustment.

With the belt-and-pulley configuration, check the belt for cracks, other signs of wear, and proper tension. If the belt is worn, replace it. (Be sure to shut off power to the furnace first.)

To check the tension, push down on the belt. It should give about ½ inch. If an adjustment is necessary, loosen the bolts securing the motor, slide the motor to a position in which the tension is correct, and retighten bolts.

## Blower Adjustments

If you have a belt-and-pulley blower drive, you can increase or decrease the speed of the blower somewhat. An increase in speed can be very advantageous when changing from the heating to air conditioning mode of operation. Since hot air rises naturally, you may not want as much force from the blower pushing hot air up into your home during the heating season. The situation reverses in the air conditioning mode.

To increase the speed of the blower, loosen the set screw on the outside half of the motor pulley, slide it closer to the inner half, and tighten the set screw. Moving it away from the inner half decreases the blower speed.

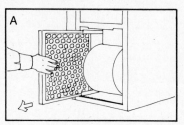
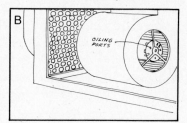
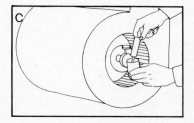
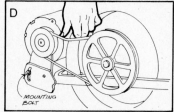

# BALANCING A FORCED-AIR SYSTEM

Today, when the ducts for a forced-air system are run, each is dampered, then the installers balance the system. But even these procedures don't guarantee the correct air flow into each room. Lots of things can throw off this balancing act; the chief of these is the exposure of or the amount of glass in a room.

In existing systems, too, you may need to balance the flow to suit your needs. You may have tried unsuccessfully to balance your air system by controlling the registers in the various rooms. That didn't work because when you closed down the damper on a room register, you did little to redi-

rect that air to other parts of the home.

To balance a system properly, you will have to work with dampers in the ducts, which are controlled by handles or locknuts (A). These dampers usually are found near where the supply ducts branch off from the furnace plenum. If your system doesn't have dampers, a heating or sheet metal contractor can install them for you.

Begin your task by studying the direction of the ducts and shutting them off one at a time. By doing this you can easily determine which ducts feed which registers. When you have all of them isolated, label each duct.

Then, tape a series of thermometers side by side on a wall and wait about a half hour. If there is any discrepancy among their temperatures, make a note of it so you can compensate accurately

for it in your later calculations.

To do the actual balancing, wait for a cold day when the furnace is running a good deal of the time. Then distribute the thermometers to various rooms. Tape them so they are approximately three feet from the floor and not directly above the registers (B).

Now, position all the duct dampers so they are fully open. The position of a damper's handle generally coincides with the position of the damper itself.

Wait about 30 minutes until the thermometers have a chance to settle, and begin your balancing act (C). Make changes in the damper settings, doing it a little at a time. Wait at least a half-hour after each adjustment so you can note the effects of each change.

You may want to balance your system for both heating and cooling. If so, mark both settings near each damper (D).

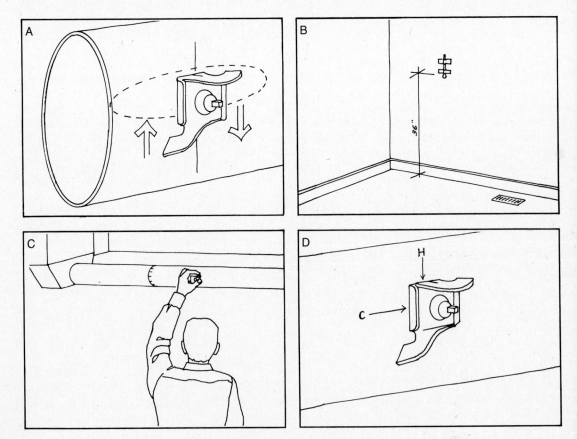

# MAINTAINING YOUR AIR CONDITIONER

As with all the rest of your space conditioning equipment, your air conditioner probably will run for years on end causing you few or no problems. And, when it does act up, it is usually a job for the professionals.

Yet, there are a few seasonal things you can do to both prolong the life of your equipment and to keep it operating at its peak efficiency.

Before attempting any maintenance, be sure no power is flowing to it. Trip the circuit breaker or unscrew the fuse at the service panel (A-1, A-2).

If you have central air, at the beginning of every cooling sea-son make sure you start out with a clean furnace filter (B). Also, oil the furnace blower and blower motor if necessary (see page 93).

Check the compressor unit, which is the portion of the system that sits outside your home. It contains condenser coils and a fan that dissipates heat from these coils. Because the compressor unit sits outside year-round, it is not uncommon for the coils to get clogged with dirt, which hinders the heat exchange process. So, be sure to clean the coils. To do this you can either hose them down through the grill on the cover (C), or if you are more industrious, you can elect to remove the cover and give the unit a more thorough cleaning.

If you take off the cover, you may want to vacuum the coils before hosing them down. But, do so with caution. These coils are made of soft metal, as are the fins attached to them. If you bend the fins, efficiency will suffer, and if you puncture the tubing the refrigerant will escape. Repair of such a leak could be costly.

While you have the cover off the compressor unit, check the fan motor housing. Some units require periodic oiling. If yours does, oil ports will be visible. A few drops of SAE 10 oil will do.

Besides the condenser coils outside your house, your central air conditioner has a similar set of coils, known as evaporator coils, indoors in a housing adjacent to your furnace. If you can get to these coils, which is not always possible, it is a good idea to gently vacuum them too (D).

There's not much maintenance involved when dealing with window air conditioners. Just keep the filter clean, oil the fan motor housing if necessary, and clean the coils occasionally.

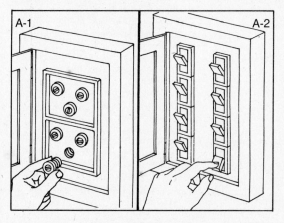

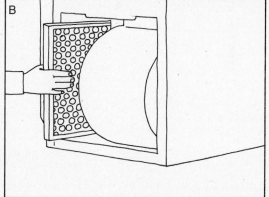

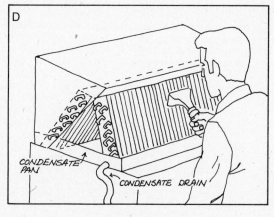

# INDEX